TABLE OF CONTENTS

FOREWORD

To be a teacher of a child who is experiencing difficulty learning in school and see in his eyes the helplessness and frustration in the face of failure is painful. But to be that child is devastating, to say the least.

Urban schools are host to an overwhelming number of students who, like the author of *Hey, Dummy,* are victims of academic failure, low self-esteem and material deprivation. Parental neglect, and in many instances, abuse, intensifies their misery. From personal experience I can attest to the profound effect of a loving, caring mother who, in the face of monumental deprivation, willingly sacrifices all for her children. There is no doubt that such was the salvation of Lonnie Clinkscale. When teachers, other children and even close family members belittled or otherwise hurt him, his mother was there to reassure him of her love for him.

The story *Hey, Dummy* is a testimonial to a lifelong dedication to the principle that all children can learn. Jim Rozzi, as I knew him, did not just believe the notion, but with enormous energy he dedicated his entire professional life to teaching, encouraging and fostering in children a sense of self-worth. To observe this marvelous teacher with students was to experience an exercise of genuine concern and determination to see them succeed. He and his assistant, Thelma Barnes, were a team for more than ten years, and together they helped children overcome learning problems and move ahead to successful school experiences.

Today, able to face audiences of school children, university professors or the clergy, public gatherings, television or radio, Lonnie Clinkscale humbly attributes his accomplishments to God working through the people who touched his life. He was able to overcome the unkindness of thoughtless teachers, with their expressions of exasperation at his inability to learn, the brutality of classmates who called him "Dummy," and the harshness of the circumstances of his early life by holding tenaciously to a strong religious faith.

As I observed Lonnie at his book signing session, I saw an unassuming, yet confident young man, who will make a positive impact not only upon the lives of readers of his book, but also upon those who bought his book and shook his hand. I am one of them.

Martha S. Bruce-McSwain

Martha K. Bruce-McSwain, Ph.D.

DEDICATION

I dedicate this book to the glory of Almighty God whose unconditional love has healed my hurts and disappointments, and who has forgiven my mistakes. Because His transforming, healing power ministered to me, through His willing servants and much prayer, I am no longer the dummy I was told I would always be.

I also dedicate this book to...
• my mother who has struggled for many years to remain an example for her children;
• my wife Paulette who, through her patience and understanding, has been my inspiration— this book would not have been written had it not been for her support and prayers;
• and to all the instructors in my motivation classes who did not give up on me, but persistently helped me gain confidence and overcome the inferiority brought upon me by my many learning disabilities.

Some of the names in this autobiography have been changed to avoid offending anyone.

Chosen Vessel
by Mrs. B. V. Cornwall Phifer

The Master was searching for a vessel to use;
On the shelf there were many — which one would he
    choose?
"Take me," cried the gold one, "I'm shiny and bright,
I'm of great value and I do things just right.
My beauty and luster will outshine the rest
And for someone like you, Master, gold would be best."

The Master passed on with no word at all;
He looked at a silver urn, narrow and tall.
"I'll serve you, dear Master, I'll pour out your wine,
And I'll be at your table whenever you dine.
My lines are so graceful, my carvings so true,
And silver will always compliment you."

Unheeding, the Master passed on to the brass.
It was wide mouthed and shallow, and polished like
    glass.
"Here! Here!" cried the vessel. "I know I will do!
Place me on your table for all men to view."

"Look at me," called the goblet of crystal so clear.
"My transparency shows my contents so dear.
Though fragile am I, I will serve you with pride,
And I'm sure I'll be happy in your house to abide."

The Master came next to a vessel of wood.
Polished and carved, it solidly stood.
"You may use me, dear Master," the wooden bowl said.
"But I'd rather you used me for fruit, not for bread."

Then the Master looked down and saw a vessel of clay.
Empty and broken it helplessly lay.
No hope had the vessel that the Master might choose,
To cleanse and make whole, to fill and to use.

"Ah! This is the vessel I've been hoping to find.
I will mend and use it and make it all mine.

"I need not the vessel with pride of its self;
Nor the one who is narrow to sit on the shelf;
Nor one who is bigmouthed and shallow and loud;
Nor one who displays his contents so proud.
Not the one who thinks he can do all things just right,
But this plain vessel filled with my power and might."

Then gently He lifted the vessel of clay,
Mended and cleansed it, filled it that day,
Spoke to it kindly, "There's work you must do.
Just pour out to others as I pour out to you."

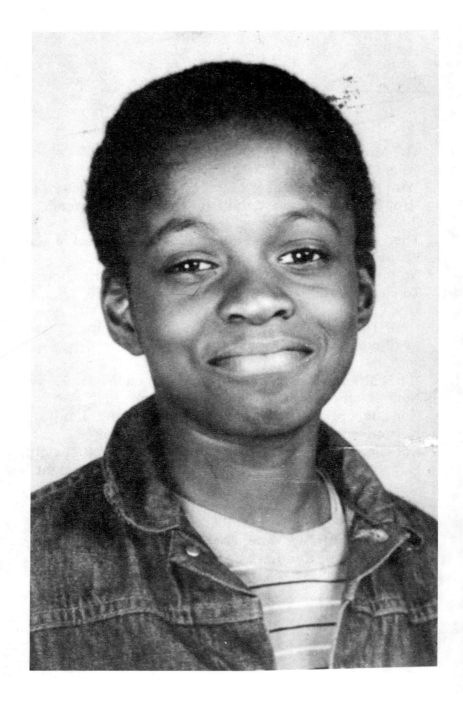

Chapter 1
School Daze

"Lonnie Clinkscale."

"Y-y-y-yes M-m-m-m-maam?" The other children in my first grade class, amused over my inability to speak without stuttering, began to snicker as usual. A boy in the front row could not contain his amusement and burst into a full-fledged giggle.

"Lonnie, go to the blackboard and print your name."

"Y-y-y-yes M-m-maam." I couldn't bear to look up as I arose from my assigned seat in the farthest corner of the class room and walked toward the front chalkboard. Hesitantly I picked up the long piece of chalk from the dusty chalk tray and printed L, then O... For the life of me, I couldn't remember what came next.

One of my classmates whispered, "What a dummy! He can't even spell his own name!" Someone else unsuccessfully tried to suppress a giggle. I turned and looked toward my teacher, hoping she would give me some small sign of encouragement.

Instead, she heaved a sigh of exasperation and, taking the chalk from my hand, wrote on the board, high above my head, "2+2=." "Lonnie," she said as she placed the chalk in the palm of my hand, "write the answer to that problem."

My mind swirled. I could not think. Yet I knew if I did not give an answer the whole class would laugh at me. After a brief

silence which seemed like hours, knowing everyone was waiting for me to respond, the number 5 came to my mind. *That's
it!* I thought to myself. *That must be the answer! 2+2=5!* Quickly
I stood on my tiptoes and stretched my arm as far as I could to
place my answer in its proper place. Finally I would do
something right and receive acceptance from my teacher and
my classmates.

To my dismay, the moment I wrote the number 5, the whole
class exploded into hysterics and the teacher cupped her hand
over her mouth to hide her own laughter. I turned and began the
long torturous journey to my rightful position in the back
corner of the room.

"Dummy!" one of the children called out as I hurried to get
to the safety of my seat behind every one else. "Hey, dummy!"

"What a dumbbell!" added another. I cringed and strained
to walk faster.

The teacher interrupted their name-calling. "Let's get on
with more important things," she said loudly, waving her hand
for silence. The class returned to order. I heard nothing that
followed.

*Why didn't she make them stop their laughing and name
calling?* I wondered. *I know now why she makes me sit in the
back corner of the room. She's ashamed of me. I'm the least
important member of this class!*

This pattern of being assigned to a special seat away from
the other students because I was unable to speak clearly,
unable to think and remember, followed me throughout the
elementary grades. The laughter and ridicule followed as well.

My appearance was another source of mockery. Coming
from a family of six children— four girls and two boys, and I was
a twin in number three position— I did not have nice clothes like
the other children had. Every day I had to wear the same worn
out hand-me-downs and the same shoes with gaping holes in
the sides and torn soles. Because my mother was already at
work when I left for school, I had no one to teach me about the
importance of keeping myself clean.

During recess, I played alone. The other children refused to
play with a kid who was too dumb to spell his own name. When
I came near, they clustered in little groups and turned their
backs. I felt so rejected and unloved— a nobody.

I might have been relieved to hear the bell that signaled the close of the school day if it had not been for the dreaded walk home. I always tried to be the first or the last to leave the building so I wouldn't have to be near the other children because, as I walked home, many of the students made a game of pushing me around and laughing at me.

One day while I was in the cafeteria line and the children were making fun of me as usual, one young man who was known as The Bully and was popular with the girls made sarcastic statements about me.

"Look at Lonnie!" He pointed toward my feet and howled with laughter. "He got holes in his shoes! Hey, it must be raining out—look at Lonnie's pants. He got on high waters!"

What seemed to be an intolerably deafening roar of laughter echoed throughout the cafeteria. I felt I could take no more. In my frustration I picked up a chair and ran after him. A couple of the teachers on duty restrained me until I could calm down.

Every time it was my turn to read, knowing I would be laughed at because of my speech impediment, I fixed my eyes on a selected spot on the floor and stuttered until I could hardly be understood. I didn't dare to look up, knowing I would see the expressions of amusement on the children's faces. I interpreted the teacher's smile to mean that she was thinking, *Oh, boy, here we go again!* I was not so dumb that I was unable to detect their opinions of me.

Noticing that during reading class I was always given the shortest assignment, I was certain that my elementary teachers were ashamed of me because of my learning disabilities. I was never selected for an important class responsibility or for participation in special projects, holiday programs and school plays. If I did have a part, I always got backstage work, such as rearranging the stage after the curtain was pulled.

When my class was asked to recite for special guests who came to the school from time to time I was never given a part. The message was clear. The role I was to play was, "Good little Lonnie, stay in your corner in the back of the room and be quiet."

Chapter 2
Convinced

One day— I think it was when I was in the third grade— the principal came into our classroom and whispered something into our teacher Miss Walker's ear. She nodded her approval. He then announced, "Children, your class has been selected to perform a play entitled 'Mr. Scrooge.' This is a special honor, so you must do your best. You will have to give three performances because I plan to invite your parents, grandparents and the whole community. I have also invited the superintendent of schools, plus other school-related dignitaries. I have instructed Miss Walker to make sure each one of you has a special part."

For several days the teacher read the play out loud to familiarize us with the story. I trembled each time she read about Mr. Scrooge's coffin being rolled to center stage. To me it was the most important moment in the play. The high point.

All my fellow class mates were so excited the day Miss Walker announced, "Class, I believe we know the story well enough now for me to assign the parts." In spite of the principal's insistence that everyone should have a part, I knew I would be left out.

Squeals of delight filled our classroom each time the teacher read off the name of a character in the play and the name of the student who would be taking that part. After all the speaking parts had been given out, Miss Walker looked at me and stated, "Lonnie, even you will have a part in this play. Your responsibility will be to roll Mr. Scrooge's coffin across the stage when the proper signal is given."

I felt good! I had been given an important responsibility! For the first time I was accepted as part of my class. *Maybe a change was taking place,* I thought. Certainly new light was shining on my perception of my classmates and my teacher. *Maybe they didn't think as little of me as I had imagined!*

After weeks of rehearsal, the exciting day finally arrived. I hated the idea of not having a new outfit to wear for such an important occasion. Especially I dreaded not having new shoes. My older brother Eddie, who was in junior high, had given me his old pair, size 10 1/2, twice the size that I needed. I had no choice but to wear them since the sole of one of my size five oakies had come off the previous day because the heat from the sidewalk had melted the glue. They had been repaired once too often. Eddie's worn out shoes were at least in better condition than mine, so I stuffed toilet tissue in the toes for a better fit and left for school, my mind filled with visions of being congratulated by my classmates for my superb accomplishment of rolling the coffin onto the stage at just the right moment.

With only minutes left before the curtain was to go up for our first performance, our teacher, with a nervous tremor in her voice, gave us our last minute instructions. "Now, children," she concluded, "I must stress again what the principal said about doing well. You know how many school dignitaries will be watching you." I sensed our doing well would be significantly important for her also.

Some of us peeked through the curtains and our jitters instantly intensified. The school auditorium was packed wall to wall. We held our breath as the curtain slowly and ominously raised and the play began.

Everyone was performing well. Then came the most important part of the program. I watched for the signal that would indicate it was time for me to move Mr. Scrooge's open coffin to center stage. My whole class, including the teacher, had their fingers crossed.

The teacher nodded her head. That was my cue! Silence told me that my classmates and my teacher were all wishing the same thing: "Oh, I hope Lonnie doesn't mess up!" I was too nervous to look around, but sensed that everyone's eyes were on me. Was I really going to make it?

As I began to roll the cardboard coffin towards center stage I accidentally tripped over my brother's size 10 1/2 shoe and fell inside the huge box. It rolled across the stage and behind the curtain on the opposite side.

The entire auditorium was filled with an uproar of laughter as the school principal and the teacher helped me back to my feet. I was mortified, devastated. I felt like a nerd. I had cheapened the most serious part of the play into a comedy. Words could not describe my feelings of having let down my teacher and my classmates. More important, I felt I had let myself down as well. For the first time I KNEW everything the teachers and students had said was right. I *am a dummy!* my heart screamed inside of me. *I'll never be anything in life!*

After the play was over and we had returned to our class room, Miss Walker leaned against the front of her desk and announced, "Children, I'm so proud of you!" She looked every child in the eye. "You did well!"

Then, her gaze shifted to the back corner of the room and centered on me. For the first time she showed open anger and frustration towards me. "Lonnie, I have never been so embarrassed in my entire life! The description 'Dumbbell' fits you well!"

The entire class roared with laughter, reinforcing every thought that had been racing through my mind. "Dumbbell! Stupid!"

Then our teacher announced, "Paul, for the last two performances you will take the coffin out on the stage." Tears streamed down my cheeks. My heart was broken. Even though I had tried my best to please my classmates and my teacher, I had failed.

I was returned to my customary responsibilities behind the curtain. "Lonnie, bring the chair out when I tell you and then keep off the stage."

All the way home that fateful day, children followed me, jeering, "Hey, dummy! You messed up our play! You messed up our play!" By the time I arrived home, my sisters and brother had already heard about my fiasco. It was difficult for them to understand my situation, because, although my brother had to struggle to some degree, my sisters had no difficulty making it through school. None of them were ever held back. How I wished I could be like my sister Sherri who was a top student.

The day after our final performance of "Mr. Scrooge," the teacher sent out for pizza for the entire class. When the pizza was delivered Miss Walker announced, "Here's a treat for you because you've all done so well!" The other children cheered.

That pizza looked so good, and smelled even better. I could have eaten four or five pieces in nothing flat. At our home we never knew what the word "pizza" meant. We never knew what the word "hot dog" meant. The only thing we knew about was grits, beans and oatmeal.

Suddenly the cheering stopped and my classmates all turned to look with disgust toward my place in the back corner of the room. I felt they were wondering if I would have nerve to take a slice. In my ankle-high jeans and size 10 1/2 tennis shoes, I stared at the floor and struggled to remain very still and quiet, hoping I would not attract further adverse attention. Although the teacher did not tell me I was not allowed to have a piece, I could not bring myself to eat a single bite of the reward for a job well done.

Troubled about what Miss Walker had said about my being a dumbbell, I ached to tell my parents what had happened in school that day, but was afraid I would get a spanking. Besides, I did not want to approach my parents because I knew they must have had more important things on their minds than to listen to someone as insignificant as I. I hated being from a large family. My interpretation of my home situation only added to my difficulties and drove me to withdraw and become a loner.

Even as I went on to fourth grade the following year the students never let me forget the incident. Any time our class gave a play, I was not allowed to participate. Always, if I had any responsibility, it was backstage after the curtains were closed.

Chapter 3
Life at Home

Regularly both my parents tried to help me with my school work. "Lonnie, come sit at the kitchen table. What's two plus two?" my father would ask. "If you have two oranges and I give you two more oranges, how many do you have?"

Usually I was afraid to give an answer for fear it would not be correct, but in many cases I did not know the correct answer. The harder I tried, the less I could comprehend or remember. It hurt me to see expressions of frustration and anger on my parents' faces. I became more and more withdrawn and afraid to go to them for help. The last thing I wanted to do was upset my parents. I loved them both so deeply and wanted nothing more than to make them proud of me.

After my father looked at my report card at the end of my first year of school and saw that I had been held back, he was so disappointed that, without thinking, he said, "Lonnie, you'll never be anything in life. You'll never be like your sisters."

When I returned to school in the fall, his words still rang in my mind. His words "You'll never make it" haunted my thoughts. I was convinced I would never be successful in school, in life, in relationships. There was no hope for me.

Although my father was a great provider, I never felt I really knew him because he worked long hours in the steel mill or was laid off and had to work several odd jobs. He always made sure the bills were paid and we had food in the house— even if it was only oatmeal or beans.

Although I sensed he loved his children, I never knew my father to tell any of us, "I love you." I cannot remember my father having the time to take any of us to a football game or to see a school play. As a child, my father had a very hard life and little time to play, because his father died when he was nine years old, so he was faced with the responsibility of taking care of his mother. He never had a chance to have a normal childhood.

As I grew older I began to understand that perhaps, since he did not have a father figure in the home to teach him how to spend time with his children, he didn't know how to fulfill the role himself or how to express his love. The few times that my father and I spent together are now cherished memories.

I was especially thrilled the day he took his family to the drive-in theater to see "The Ten Commandments." We all packed lunches and climbed into the car, surprised that our father was taking the time to be with us.

At intermission, he opened the door on the driver's side of the car. "Where are you going, Daddy?" we all clammered. "Where are you going?"

"I'm going to buy you some popcorn," he explained. While he was in the concession building, with children's high-pitched voices of excitement, we chattered in wonderment about this unusual experience. When our Daddy returned, his arms were loaded with not only popcorn, but hot dogs for everyone. We were ecstatic!

Soon the movie began again and in serious tones our father explained the meaning and importance of living by the Ten Commandments. I was touched by his attempt to instill in us the desire to be good children.

I'll never forget the time our TV broke and my father proceeded to fix it. "Lonnie, come here," he said without looking up from his project. "I'll show you how to fix this TV." I hurried to his side as he took the back cover off the floor-model television set.

He pointed to the center of the TV and said, "This large tube is known as the picture tube. It is very expensive to replace it.

Once this tube is no longer working, Son, it would be best to replace the entire TV." I nodded that I understood.

He continued, "See the tube on the right that has a big black spot in the middle?"

"Yes," I replied.

"That tube is known as the power tube. The black spot tells me that it has burned out and that is the reason why the TV would not come on." He pulled out a new power tube from his TV repair kit, which was filled with various sizes and shapes of replacement tubes. "Here, Lonnie, have the honor of installing this new tube."

My eyes lit up with excitement when I saw that I had been able to repair the set so that a clear picture came on the screen once again. I was delighted that my father took the time to show me how to repair the problem.

I also remember, when I was about ten years old, he said to me, "Lonnie, let's go get something to eat." To my delight he took me to a restaurant and bought me a hot dog and some french fries. I really felt good! *This is MY father,* I thought to myself and knew that deep down inside him was a love for me he was unable to express.

My father was a stern disciplinarian who believed in having an orderly household. Spankings were his main mode of discipline. If one child did something wrong, we all were spanked. He felt all six of us knew what had gone wrong and were therefore responsible.

One day, as he relaxed in his swivel chair with his back turned toward the kitchen door, I snitched his jar of peanuts off the kitchen counter. He swirled around just in time to catch me in the act and ordered me to sit in my little sister's high chair in the kitchen. I trembled as I watched him form a hat out of a piece of newspaper.

"This is a dummy hat, Lonnie. Every time one of your brothers or sisters come through the kitchen door, you tell them 'My name is Lonnie. I am a dummy. I am a peanut thief.' You MUST learn not to steal." My mother came home from work just in time to rescue me from my degrading punishment.

I realize now that my father's intent had been to spur me on to do better work in school. He had wanted me to be an obedient son and do well and was extremely disappointed that I had not.

Throughout much of my childhood my mother worked three jobs. She was a cleaning lady for the school system at night. She would leave that job and go to a nearby bank building and clean for a couple of hours. On weekends she washed walls and provided maid service for a wealthy family. She did not have as much time to spend with her children as she would have liked, and many times fell asleep as she tried to talk with us after a hard day's work.

On Sunday mornings she lined up her six children like little soldiers to walk them to church. Even though I hated school, I looked forward to going to church, perhaps because I felt that, at church, people looked beyond my shortcomings. The love and acceptance I found there provided a warm and caring family-like atmosphere. Mother was troubled that I could not pronounce my words or read. On her days off she frequently went to the school to see how her children were doing and talked with my teachers to find out how she might help tutor me at home.

I have many painful recollections of the children in school making fun of the way my mother dressed, since she usually got her clothes and ours from the Good Will Store or from the rich folks whose house she cleaned.

Even though I hated having only three shabby pairs of pants and my big brother's shoes to wear, I knew that my mother was doing the best she could do to provide for her family.

Chapter 4
Anything for Attention

At times, in the days that followed the Scrooge crisis, I thought I detected that Miss Walker was sorry she had expressed such extreme anger toward me. After the pizza party was over, I sensed her attempts to be more compassionate, but that only lasted until I convinced her, through my inability to learn and my stuttering, that I truly was hopeless.

Actually, I had become too afraid to give an answer, because I was convinced it would be wrong anyway. It was painful to see the same expression of helplessness and frustration on her face that I had so often seen on my parents' faces.

Now I realize that she was an excellent teacher who was totally frustrated with her student who, no matter how much she tried to help, was not comprehending the material.

I would be dishonest if I did not mention that, although a couple of my earlier grade-school teachers were impatient with my difficulties, several of the others tried to be understanding and helpful. But the damage had been done. I knew that when a new school year began, my teacher for that year had to be thinking, *Oh, no, here comes Lonnie.* No matter how kind the teacher was, I was convinced I was a hopeless dummy.

I felt rejected by the children in my class each time they

laughed at me or picked on me. I interpreted being assigned each year to a seat in the back of the room, separate from the rest of the class, to mean that none of my teachers wanted to be bothered with me. And, most important of all, I was convinced I was not loved by my four sisters and my brother, or by my parents. I remained in a state of anger. No one had the time to help me. Nobody cared.

One day, when I was nine or ten years old, I dashed out of the school building as quickly as I could to avoid walking home with the other children and noticed an old brown Chevy parked in front of the school playground. The driver waved his arm out of the window and called out to me, "Hey, kid. Come here." Something within warned me to ignore him, so I walked by with caution. "Kid! Don't you want to feel good?" Curiosity forced me to turn my head. He opened a small package and held it out toward me. "Here, try this. If you want more, I'll supply it for you and for your school friends for a small fee." I could not resist accepting his offer.

The yellow package I took from his hand contained a powdery substance. For some reason, I was certain that if I took that substance it would make me ill, but I didn't care. I thought, *If I take this stuff and get sick, I might finally receive some love and attention from my parents. Maybe my fellow classmates won't make fun of me anymore. Maybe, instead, they'll feel sorry for me.*

I ran down the street and hid behind the bushes in a nearby yard where I swallowed the substance. By the time I reached my home, I was so dizzy I began to bump into walls.

"Lonnie, what's the matter with you?" my mother asked with alarm. I could only mutter incoherently. "Here, son, stay on the couch until your father comes home from work. We'll have to take you to the hospital to see what's wrong with you."

The hospital attendants pumped my stomach and ran a lot of unpleasant tests.

As my father sat on the edge of my bed, he explained to me, "Whatever you ate, Lonnie, it made you very sick." I was hospitalized for one month. My parents' daily visits warmed my heart. In the confines of my hospital room I had them all to myself. I never told them why I took that substance.

When I was released from the hospital I didn't mind returning to school because I believed that, having gone through such an ordeal, I would receive more respect from my teacher and my fellow students. And I was certain my parents would continue to give me more attention.

As the days passed I found that my dream had come true. My parents checked on me regularly, asking "How do you feel, Lonnie? Are you feeling okay?" My teachers, through a program in the school system, arranged for me to have brand-new clothes— several pairs of pants, a couple pairs of tennis shoes, and some bright new shirts.

My plan worked, I thought with delight. *It was worth it all!*

Too soon my teacher wrote a simple math problem on the blackboard and asked, "Lonnie, do you feel well enough to come up and write the correct answer to this problem?" I found I was still unable to read, write or comprehend what my teacher had asked me to do. Once again, to my dismay, the other children laughed at me and, dejected, I returned to my assigned seat at the back of the classroom.

Chapter 5
Motivated to Improve

For the life of me I did not understand why I could not spell my name or add two plus two. It seemed I was unable to hear what the teacher was saying, but hearing tests revealed no problem. Was there some kind of blockage in my mind? I wonder, now that I have been taught in the ways of the Church, if I had been hindered by a evil spirit which had blocked my ability to think or speak clearly.

By the time I was ready to enter the fourth grade, my teachers were frustrated because they found they were spending more time teaching me than the rest of the class and yet were making little if any progress. Finally they suggested to the Board of Education that I should be registered in special motivation classes which had been established to help students overcome learning disabilities in reading, writing, math and speech. The Board called my mother and asked her to come to the school so they could tell her about the recommendation. She agreed and signed the necessary papers.

I began to attend these special classes two days out of each school week and soon felt more at ease, since I was among children who had problems similar to mine. I was relieved and comforted to discover I was not the only child in the world who had learning disabilities.

A second discovery was quite painful. On days I was to go to motivation class, not long after the lunch hour was over, my teacher would always say, "Lonnie, it's your time." I would then leave my regular class room and go to the special class. Soon the other children realized where I was going, and when the teacher would tell me it was time to leave, my class mates would turn and grin at me with raised eyebrows. I was intimidated.

Some snickered, "He's goin' to the retard class!"

"Well, he *is* retarded. That's why he's going."

"Yeh, those classes are for the dummies!"

Just before the end of the school day I returned to my regular class. Again, the children in the room would stare and grin.

In spite of feeling ill at ease over the reaction of my classmates, I enjoyed attending Motivation and LAMPS (I don't remember what the letters represent, but I always interpreted it to mean shedding a light into the lives of those who had learning disabilities). The teachers were very understanding and proceeded at a slower pace, spending more time on each subject and taking time with each child.

I especially liked the incentive programs. If a child got so many mathematical problems correct, or read so many books he or she was awarded tokens which could be used to buy candy, pencils, notebooks, etc., at the "store" within the classroom. At home, candy was a delicacy. To possess my own brand-new notebooks and pencils was a great incentive to strive harder.

I recall Mr. James Rozzi spending much time helping me overcome my reading problems. An excellent teacher, Mr. Rozzi went beyond the call of duty. I wish there were more teachers as concerned and dedicated as he and his assistants.

During my first week in Motivation Class I was instructed by Mr. Rozzi to begin reading a short paragraph from The *Daily Reader*, a book consisting of short stories. I was so nervous and afraid I would be laughed at that I could not even pronounce a single word.

Mr. Rozzi walked over to me and placed his right hand on my left shoulder. In a soft gentle voice he advised, "Lonnie, take your time. You can do it. I know you can." His gentle words of encouragement instilled in me the confidence and self-esteem that I so badly needed.

He often took time after school to work with me in order to help me overcome my learning disabilities in reading. At the conclusion of our time together he drove me home.

A caring environment of acceptance and patience was created by his gentle voice, his confidence and determination. I began to look forward to going to school.

Also, I remember Mrs. Barnes' helpfulness. I learned through Motivation and LAMPS classes that there were teachers who were concerned about their students and their students' futures.

Miss Burney, teacher of my regular fourth-grade class, frequently made plans to pick me up at my home on Friday or Saturday afternoon to rake leaves at her home or do various other chores for her. She spent a lot of time trying to tutor me and paid me for my help or bought me pencils and other needed school supplies.

Even though I was receiving help at school, I was receiving very little help from home.

Chapter 6
The Divorce

During the time I was attending special classes, I became a very nervous child and often went into deep depression because of my parents' frequent arguments which were mostly over finances. Since my father was away from home so much, he got very little rest. He overreacted if a bill wasn't paid on time or if the house wasn't cleaned to perfection. Many times my mother warned my sisters, my brother and me before she left for work, "Make sure you clean the house!"

One time my father announced, "There's a blueberry stain left on the kitchen counter!"and spanked all six of us. It seemed to me then that he was searching for reasons to argue, but I believe now that his frequent outbursts of anger stemmed from not being free to live his life as he would have liked. The obligation he felt to provide for his family overpowered his desire to be free.

During this time of personal struggle, my father often took my mother to buy groceries after she came home from work at night. He would firmly instruct her, "Be sure you stay right here at the store until I come back to get you." Many times he would not return for several hours. By the time they came home, we children would have fallen asleep without any supper. No matter how late it was, Mother always fixed a meal and woke us up to eat.

I must have been in fifth or sixth grade when my mother and father had a severe fight. I heard my father scream at my mother. A moment later Mother, with tears streaming down her cheeks, ran into my bedroom, hugged me and sobbed, "That's all right. This is MY son!" I was convinced he had been complaining about me. All my parents' problems must be my fault! I agonized after she left my room. Why do I have to be so dumb? Why can't I be smart like my sisters and my brother? Why can't I talk without stuttering?

Before my father left the house one Saturday morning, he instructed my brother Eddie and me to clean the basement. Knowing what a perfectionist our father was, Eddie and I swept, scrubbed and dusted. We cleaned the floors, the steps and the walls so thoroughly we couldn't wait for Daddy to come home so see the fine job we had done.

When he returned late that evening, our father's inch-by-inch inspection of the basement revealed a couple of insignificant dusty areas our childhood eyes had missed. Both Eddie and I received sound spankings.

As I stood near the basement steps and sobbed, my pain came more from disappointment and frustration than from the spanking. I thought to myself, *No matter how much I try, I'll NEVER be able to please him! I can't live like this anymore!* I dashed up the steps and out the door into the darkness.

Horns tooted as I bolted across busy streets. Dogs barked as I scrambled through back yards and vacant lots. I was in such a confused state of mind that I didn't know where I was or where I was going.

I must have traveled in a large circle because, after what seemed like hours of stumbling through the darkness, I found myself back home. I panicked, knowing I must get out of sight before anyone saw me. *The garage! I'll hide in the garage!* I dashed in the side door and scrambled into a corner behind a pile of old tires.

When my mother came home from work around 11:30 that night, she was alarmed to learn that I had been missing for so long and began to search for me. Finally she found me huddled and trembling in my hiding place. At first I was too afraid to come out and too depressed to talk. In her usual gentle manner,

Mother coaxed until I climbed out of my sanctuary. She took me in her arms.

"This won't happen any more, Lonnie," she assured me repeatedly as we walked toward the house together. "No one will harm you again. You are very important to me. I will never stop loving and caring for you." She ushered me past my father and up to my bedroom. She tucked my covers tightly around me and kissed my forehead. "I love you, Lonnie. Get some rest now."

Mother had often soothed me by taking me in her arms and telling me how much she loved me. Those tender moments had always sustained me, but that night I was so upset I could not be comforted. I cried myself to sleep.

Some time later my father punished Eddie for something he said he didn't do. The anger which had built up in his heart from seeing our mother mistreated so often and the frustration of receiving unjust punishment caused Eddie to lose his temper. "I've got something for you, Daddy!" my teen-age brother warned during their wrestling bout and he struck his father. Somehow Daddy managed to pull away from him and call the police. In what seemed to be only moments they arrived and took my brother to the detention home.

As was her custom, my mother called from work to check on her family. My sister told her, "Dad and Eddie are fighting." Mother rushed home. When she entered the house, my father warned her, "I've sent him to the detention home and I don't want you going there to get him out. He needs to stay there for a while." In spite of the warning Mother brought Eddie home.

As my mother contemplated the toll these frequent painful incidents were taking on her family, she made up her mind she had to leave my father. In order to prevent further fighting and injury, she had to get a divorce.

The following morning my mother told all of us children, "I will not stay with your father any longer. I've made arrangements for you three oldest children to stay at grandpa and grandma's until I find a place where all of us can live together. You three younger children will have to stay here with your father for a while." Because my grandfather was very ill, my mother felt that the older children would not disturb him as much as the younger ones.

Although my grandparents' home was small, mother had no where else to go. She walked eighteen blocks to take the three oldest children to my grandmother's house. The rest of us remained with my father.

Whenever I tried to discuss with my brother and sisters my feelings about the reason for the upheaval in our family, they refused to talk with me. I had not known that in an attempt to protect me from further hurt, Mother had told them, "Whatever happens, never mention anything to Lonnie about his learning disabilities. Above all, never tease him." I was certain my sisters and brother blamed me for the separation of our parents.

Two weeks after my mother left my father, her parents drew enough money out of their bank account to pay the first month's rent on a home for her and her six children. Mother came by taxi to our father's home to get us three younger children.

As the taxi pulled away I turned around to look at my home for the last time and saw my father staring out the front picture window with tears streaming down his cheeks. It was the first time I had ever seen my father cry. He had always taught me that only girls cried. Boys did not.

MY father really does love us! I realized. *He doesn't want to see his family torn apart!* However, because of the effects of various personal incidents in his life, there was no way to avoid the separation.

We moved into an old rat-infested neighborhood on the lower south side of Youngstown. We could actually look outside through holes in the basement walls. Often we had to contact the landlord, because the bathroom drains were backed up into the basement. Yet I knew my mother was doing the best that she could.

Even though my father had spent little time with me, I missed his presence and his ability to make any necessary repairs. Just knowing he wasn't going to be around left an empty spot in my heart.

Once a month my father stopped by and my mother sent one of the oldest children out to his car to receive the money he brought to help with the rent and the other bills. His conscientiousness about being the provider for his family never diminished.

I wanted more than anything for my parents to be together again. Because of their divorce, my inability to concentrate on my school work increased markedly, even though I was still receiving tutoring from the Motivation and LAMPS classes. All I could think about was that my mother and father were separated and I was responsible.

I decided that if I were to become ill again and had to return to the hospital, I would be able to bring my father and mother back together. Late one Friday night, as I lay on my bed mulling over the plight of our family, a vision of two bottles in our medicine cabinet popped into my head. If I take all those pills and get sick again, that will bring my parents back together, I decided. Their mutual concern for me will make everything all right. I dashed down the stairs to the medicine cabinet, put the pills in my mouth and swallowed some water, but the pills refused to go down my throat. Each time I tried to take them I regurgitated. Finally I became too tired to try again and returned to my bed. I was so frustrated! What a total failure I am! I can't even successfully remove the cause of my family's devastation!

A second thought entered my mind. *Maybe I wasn't able to destroy myself because there is a purpose for my life! But what could that purpose be? Anyway, I'll never go back to that medicine cabinet again!* I never told my parents or any other member of the family what I had attempted.

Chapter 7
My Imaginary Friend

When I went to school the Monday after my parents' separation I was faced not only with sarcastic remarks about my learning disabilities, but with the news of my parents' divorce, which already had spread throughout the school. Several of the children made cruel statements such as, "Now Lonnie doesn't have a daddy."

There were times I would go home, head straight to the room I shared with my brother and cry in the darkness. In agony I would rock the bed, wishing my family was back together again.

How I wished I had somebody to talk to— someone who would understand. I talked to myself, but that didn't seem to help. I wished I could talk with my father.

There were times I would go back to our family home and cut the lawn for my father, hoping we would be able to chat, but most of the time he was not at home.

One day when I was lying on my bed, feeling especially lonely and heartbroken, I reached out to the shelf beside the bed and picked up my favorite toy, a GI Joe doll. I envisioned him as an imaginary friend who took the place of my father. He became everything I thought my father should be for me. My imaginary new friend was a great comfort. He began to tell me what to do and how to do it. Whenever I was lonely or depressed, I talked to him and in my mind received advice about how to do my chores and what to do in school.

Soon, holding the doll was unnecessary. By using my

imagination I could have any kind of friend I wanted or needed at any given moment. My imaginary friend was always one who was strong and mighty and well-liked by everyone. He was great in sports and someone children admired. He was well-liked by my teachers and classmates, had plenty of money and fancy clothes.

I envisioned my imaginary friend giving my mother plenty of money and putting her into a big beautiful house so she would no longer have to worry about scrubbing floors and washing walls to make a meager living.

What started out to be an innocent means of release grew into an obsession. More and more this companion filled the void that had been created by my father's absence. I could not exist without him. I never named him, but would call him by the name of whomever I wanted to have as my friend that particular day. If I had seen someone in school who was popular or did well in his studies and wished I could be like him, I would call my friend by the name of that person. If I thought of Joey who was good in sports, I imagined my friend was also good in sports and called him Joey for the rest of the day.

Every day I could not wait to go home from school just to talk to my imaginary friend. After supper I would run upstairs and put the lights out so I could talk to him again.

Several times my mother came into my room to ask, "Who are you talking to, Lonnie?"

"A-a-a fr-fr-friend." I found myself establishing a progressive dependency upon my imaginary friend. As I saw less of my father and the imaginary friend began to take his place I became more of a loner. If my imaginary friend told me in my mind to be stubborn in school, or not to listen to the teacher, I would do whatever he said to do.

Nearly every day, as I entered the school building, boys jumped me. While they held me down, they asked, "Hey, dummy, you got any money on you?"

"N-n-no!" I would answer. "O-o-only m-m-my l-l-lunch."

"O-o-only m-m-my l-l-lunch," they would mimic, then grab my lunch and run down the hall, laughing.

Finally, one night my imaginary friend awakened me and said, "Tomorrow when you go to school, fight 'em!" I got into various brawls because my friend told me to fight back instead of letting the children boss me around. I felt I had power and control of my destiny.

My friend began to speak to me in dreams. He was very strong and muscular and encouraged me in my dreams to fight with the people who had upset me during the day. "I'll be right there to back you up," he said. The bullies at school began to leave me alone.

"Something's happened to Lonnie. He's not the same," they said with amazement. "We'd better not pick on him any more."

I then became bold and rebellious, to a point where my friend caused me to dream I could steal whatever I wanted from the teacher's desk and purse. I can recall telling the teacher, "I-I-I'm n-n-not f- f-feeling w-w-well. W-w-will it b-b-be all r-r-right if I j-j-just r- r-rest m-m-my h-h-head on the d-d-desk wh-wh-while the other ch-ch- children g-g-go to r-r-recess?"

She gave me permission to remain in the room. I then stole money from her purse. My success and the urging of my imaginary friend encouraged me to take whatever I could from her desk and from the children's coat pockets in the cloak room. This was the beginning of my having not only disability problems but also personality problems. Constantly my mother had to go to the school to discuss my behavior with my teacher.

It was not difficult for the teacher to quickly catch on that my frequent illnesses coincided with missing items. One particular day she set me up.

"I-I-I'm ill ag-g-gain t-t-today, M-m-miss Br-br-brown. M-m-may I p-p-please s-s-stay in fr-fr-from r-r-recess ag-g-gain t-t-today?"

"Why, sure, Lonnie," she responded. I cradled my head in my arm on the desk until I was sure the teacher had gone out of the room. Then I walked to her desk. My eyes lit up at a heavenly sight! Carefully arranged in a neat row on Miss Brown's desk were the most beautiful colored marking pens I had ever seen. Quickly I grabbed them and ran to the cloak room. I stuffed them in my coat.

When the other children returned from recess, I could hardly wait for the school day to end so I could go home and draw pictures with my new markers. Finally Miss Brown announced, "Children, it's time to go home. Get your coats on."

With enthusiasm I joined my classmates in the cloak room. Soon, in spite of the chatter and usual jostling, we were dressed to go home and stood in our assigned places in line.

When the bell rang, Miss Brown opened the door and the class began to file out of the room. Just as I was about to walk through the door, I felt Miss Brown's hand grip my shoulder. "Lonnie, stick around for a moment. I need to talk with you."

Nervously I stepped out of the way of the remaining departing children. When the last student had gone, the teacher looked at me with stern eyes. "Okay, Lonnie, where are my magic markers?"

"Wh-wh-what m-m-magic m-m-mark-k-kers?"

"You know, Lonnie. The ones you took off my desk. Remember?"

"I-i-i-n m-m-my c-c-coat." The markers had been used for bait!

She called my mother and I received a spanking when I got home. But the punishment did not diminish the power and control I felt I possessed, because I knew there had been a time I would not have been bold enough to do such a thing. I was convinced that my imaginary friend's words "You can control people" were true. Again and again he told me, "You used to be the one who was laughed at. Everyone had control over you. Now you can reverse the situation. You can make people react." I felt I had succeeded in manipulating the teacher and the system.

I believed my imaginary friend was helping me to get back at the school system and the world for the way they had treated me. He took more and more control of my life. At last I could not make any decision without my imaginary friend.

He taught me to be a master of manipulation. If I wanted more milk with my lunch, under his direction I told the teacher I'd had no breakfast and the cafeteria monitors gave me an extra carton of milk. If I wanted an extra nickel I told my teacher, "W-w-we d-d-don't have n-n-no f-f-food at h-h-home." Through the advice of my imaginary friend I learned to manipulate my fellow classmates out of food and school supplies. For the first time in my life I was able to tell people what to do and they did it.

One night in a dream my friend said, "When you go to school tomorrow, get smart with the teacher in your Motivation class." The next day, when the time came for the teacher to give out assignments for chores, I was given the task of cleaning off the tables and putting the paints away. I refused to cooperate.

"You do what I told you to do," he insisted. To his surprise, I refused again and he commented to no one in particular, "Well, how do you like those green apples?"

My friend told me, "Tell him you don't like green apples, you like red apples." I did, and the teacher stared at me in shock.

He sent a letter to my home to inform my mother about my disrespectful talk and for one day I was not permitted to participate in any class activities or earn tokens to buy pencils, tablets of paper or candy, a painful punishment for me to bear.

April 14, 1976

Mr. and Mrs. Edward Clinkscale
628 Ridge
Youngstown, Ohio   44502

Dear Mr. and Mrs. Clinkscale,

On behalf of Princeton Junior High School, the faculty and student body, we would like to extend our congratulations to you and your family for the outstanding job that Lonnie did during the recent Speech Contest in Austintown.

Lonnie is a tribute and an attribute to Princeton Junior High School. Please accept our appreciation for a job well done.

Sincerely yours,

Richard DeVincentis,
Principal

Robert Thorne,
Speech Teacher

James Rozzi,
Speech Teacher

Chapter 8
My Friend, the Enemy

When my imaginary friend showed me in my dreams the fancy late- model cars he owned and the beautiful women he attracted, I became so uncomfortable I frantically rocked my head back and forth on my pillow in an effort to escape. Often I felt like I was in a deep sleep and could not wake up, like I was trying to get up and escape but couldn't. It seemed that I could not breathe because something was on my chest trying to get inside me. The small remaining part of me that wanted to do good and right no longer had any control. My friend was an over-powering reality, like a real person who never left me alone. The bad and the wrong had taken over.

Often mother came to my room in the middle of the night and whispered in my ear, "Lonnie, are you all right?"

"Y-y-yeh," I always mumbled.

"You must have been dreaming. You were making such strange sounds! They woke me up."

During the day, without warning, I exploded into unexplainable fits of rage. Often, at the bidding of my friend, I threw objects across the room. Luckily, I never hurt anyone.

My sister was terrified one morning when, as she walked by the bathroom door, she saw me staring into the mirror with an evil look on my face. For years she was too frightened to tell anyone.

"It wasn't you, Lonnie," she admitted to me recently. "It was someone else looking out of your eyes. I was so terrified I closed the door and hid until you came out."

In spite of the sense of foreboding I felt about this so-called friend, I was convinced I could not exist without him. I became so dependent on him that each night I gently rolled my head back and forth in order to relax and get to sleep so I could escape into my dreams to meet him.

One evening while my family was together in the living room, my friend told me, "Get on the floor and start acting like a dog. Start barking. Start rolling over. Growl at people." Compulsively I dropped to the floor and began to bark.

"Lonnie, whatever is wrong with you?" my mother asked, becoming very concerned. Without success she tried to stop my bizarre behavior. "I'm calling your father. You need to go to the hospital and be examined!" She phoned my father and he rushed to our home and drove my mother and me to the emergency room at South Side Hospital.

After filling out the necessary papers, my parents and I were escorted into a small cubicle where I was told to sit on the bed. As soon as the attending nurse left the room, my father turned to my mother and motioned for her to leave us alone. When she had gone, my father leaned toward me and asked in a soft tone of voice, "Lonnie, are you serious, or are you playing with Daddy?"

"Ruff, ruff!," I responded, hoping he would give me the love and attention I craved instead of spankings. I was determined to stick to my guns to accomplish my goal.

After the child psychologist conducted a series of tests, he asked me, "Why did you bark like a dog?"

"M-m-my im-m-magin-n-nary f-f-friend t-t-told m-m-me to," I told him.

"Wait in the waiting room, please," he instructed and escorted me to the door, then asked my mother and father to come into his office. I could overhear him tell my parents, "Lonnie is exhibiting this unnatural behavior because he wants attention. He needs to be kept busy with various chores and activities. It's a natural thing for an intelligent child to have an imaginary friend, but unusual for a slow learner like your son. I can't understand how a child with his learning disabilities can have a vivid and active imagination comparable to the more brilliant children his age."

The doctor did not detect that my friend had become a reality I could not control. He suggested to my parents, "I think Lonnie should come in for a series of appointments so I can evaluate his condition."

Every time I met with the doctor, my friend instructed me, "He's not in control, you are. Laugh at him." I always did what he said.

During my appointments throughout the weeks that followed, the doctor asked me myriads of questions, gave me various tests and asked me to describe pictures he drew. Each time, my friend instructed me to give answers that were not my own.

The psychologist showed me a picture of a leaf and asked, "Lonnie, what do you interpret this to be?"

"Anyone w-w-with c-c-common sense w-w-would know th-th-that!" I responded. Then, in spite of my speech impediment, at the direction of my imaginary friend, I described in detail the type of tree the leaf had come from, a description far more detailed than the average child would have given.

The sessions concluded by the psychiatrist informing my parents, "Lonnie is okay. He's just going through a stage which is a normal for a child of his age."

My mother tried to keep me occupied by insisting that I attend the nearby Baptist church and Sunday school every Sunday and by urging me to participate in the church choir. My brother Eddie offered to let me work with him cutting lawns for $2 a day and I gave my mother half of everything I earned.

When Eddie received a job working full time at a restaurant, he informed his lawn customers that I would be taking over for him and would run errands and do the various odd jobs they might request. I received 50 cents for going to the store and taking Mrs. Swindale's trash out every Tuesday morning.

My new responsibilities made me feel really important and for the first time in months I became too occupied with my work to spend much time with my imaginary friend. When I went to bed, I was so tired I immediately dropped into a sound sleep.

Miss White, one of my customers, soon informed her friend Mrs. Boston of the good job I was doing for her, so Mrs. Boston, an elderly widow, asked me to perform various duties around her house and to run errands.

No matter how much money I made, I continued to give Mother half and save the other half. I saved enough to buy my own school clothes, so my mother only had to worry about shopping for my sisters. I was so proud of myself! I was becoming the man of the house. A new self worth was beginning to bud.

Finally I saved up so much money, I was able to buy a second- hand lawn mower from Big Bill's Lawn Care for $40. I established a larger clientele, and was able to relieve my mother of some of her financial burdens.

Also, I became more active in the church. It was a good feeling to make my own choice to go instead of having Mother prod me every Sunday morning. As I became more interested in understanding what it meant to have a relationship with God such as the preacher talked about every Sunday morning, I gradually lost interest in my imaginary friend, but he did not give up easily.

Every Sunday night after I came home from church, my imaginary friend told me, "I don't like you going to that church. You're spending too much time there. And you're spending too much time on your jobs, too. Why don't you stay home, here in your room, alone with me?"

The terrible dreams about being responsible for my parents breaking up began to reoccur. My imaginary friend manifested his jealousy by telling me, "After all, you ought to realize that I've been responsible for your success. I'm the one who got you the new jobs. I'm responsible for all the good things that have been happening to you. The least you could do is show your gratitude by spending a little more time with me." His persistence, like a powerful force, was taking control of my mind and soul. He revealed to me various names that I should call him, names which denoted power and authority.

As I worked for my customers my imaginary friend told me, "You're not being paid enough. Mrs. White and Mrs. Boston are taking advantage of you. To make up for it, you are to start stealing from them." Whenever either of those fine ladies sent me to the store, I either bought something for myself or kept some of the change. My success in stealing change and small items gave me the confidence to take larger items from their homes.

Our pastor often asked me to work around the church. Chocolate turtles for sale to support missions were stored in one of the classrooms. My friend urged, "Go ahead. Take a case of them." I did.

On another day, while I was mowing the pastor's lawn, my friend told me, "Take a break, Lonnie. Go over to the parsonage. On the back porch there are lots of empty pop bottles. Take them so you can return them to the store for the refund money." For some reason I can't fully explain, I was compelled to do what he said. As I walked toward the parsonage, he added, "And while you're at it, take everything you want from their back porch."

From behind the curtains of her kitchen window, the pastor's wife watched me remove the items off her porch, then, as I was leaving, came out into the yard. "Lonnie, you don't have to do that," she chided in a loving tone of voice. "If you wanted those pop bottles, all you would have had to do was ask for them and you could have had them. Lonnie, do you feel we aren't paying you enough? If so, maybe we can give you a little raise. But, Lonnie, you don't have to steal." She hugged me. Her loving manner touched my heart. I could not laugh or feel in control as I had when I was caught by my schoolteacher. Instead I felt confused, as if two forces were fighting to gain control of my life. For the first time the good force was overcoming the bad. I began to question whether or not my imaginary friend was really my friend.

Mrs. Boston had come to depend on me to do all her chores. My imaginary friend seemed to know when she received her monthly check. "Go over to Mrs. Boston's house," he would instruct me. "Tell her what you want and she will get it for you."

"I'd really like to have a bike," I told her on one of the days she received her check, and Mrs. Boston actually bought me a bike!

My imaginary friend knew how to use me to take advantage of the persons who employed me. One day Mrs. Boston told me to wash her walls while she was away. Just as I finished my chore, my friend instructed me, "Go into her attic." Although I didn't want to, I followed his instructions. "Look over there," he said and my head turned toward a small silver box. "Open it," I heard in my mind. I did, and found two loaded guns laying side by side. "Take the guns," my friend told me, "and place them in that paper bag over on Mrs. Boston's hope chest."

While I walked home, carrying the guns in the paper bag, a police cruiser slowed down beside me. The uniformed driver spotted the bag I held in my hands, stared at it with curiosity and stopped the car. My first inclination was to run as fast as I could, but inside me my imaginary friend yelled, "No! Don't run, Lonnie! I'm in control, so let me handle this. Wave to the police. And smile!"

The cruiser slowly moved forward to catch up with me. I smiled and waved. "How 're you doin' today, officer?"

"Fine, young man." He looked again at the bag I carried. I continued to smile and looked him straight in the eye. The cruiser moved on. I took the guns home and hid them under my bed.

That night I dreamed I was with my friend, who was very wealthy and wore fancy clothing. He said, "You can have lots of money and fancy clothes too, Lonnie, and your mother will no longer have to work three jobs . You could be well-liked by your classmates at school, Lonnie. All you have to do is follow my instructions. "

He then showed me in my dream a fabulous house. Only on TV had I seen such a large and beautiful dwelling. As we entered the front door, my friend assured me, "Your mother and father will live in that house if you do what I say." The room we were standing in became very cold and chills ran up and down my spine.

My imaginary friend continued, "In order for this dream to come true, you must point to your head one of the guns you took from Mrs. Boston's attic and you will spend eternity with me. Your dream of your parents coming together will then come true."

I awoke from my sleep, grabbed the .38 and pointed it toward my right temple. Guilt over causing my parents' divorce overwhelmed me. Spontaneously and without fear I immediately pulled the trigger, but the gun did not go off. I tried again, but it still would not fire. It was as though two opposing forces were battling in my bedroom, competing for my soul. In defeat,

I placed the guns back under my bed, flung my head on my pillow and stared at the ceiling for what seemed like hours.

Later that night, when my brother came home, I confided in him about what had happened. Eddie immediately took both of the guns from me and examined them. "I'll take charge of these," he said in a firm tone of voice.

"That .38 was in good working condition," he told me after he had disposed of the guns. "I don't understand why it didn't fire."

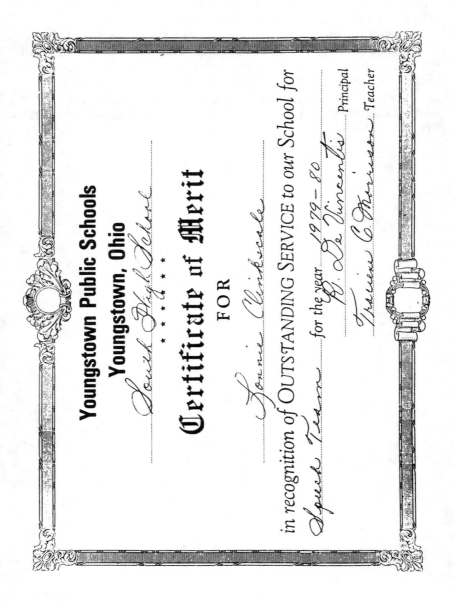

Youngstown Public Schools
Youngstown, Ohio

South High School

★ ★ ★ ★ ★

Certificate of Merit

FOR

Lonnie Chinkscale

in recognition of OUTSTANDING SERVICE to our School for

Speech Team for the year 1979–80

N. De Vincentis Principal

Florence C. Morrison Teacher

Chapter 9
I Found a New Friend.

The following night I had another dream. As I slept in my bed and my brother in his next to me, our room became a scarlet red and two angels appeared, one on the left of me and one on the right. The angel on the right spoke first.

"Lonnie, we will be with you to protect you, even unto the end of the world. If you will just put your faith in the Lord, you will be delivered from whatever problems you are experiencing in your life. The Lord wants to take you like a sculptor takes a piece of clay, and mold and shape you into the kind of person He would have you be. You now have a learning disability and are considered functionally illiterate, and you now have a very bad speech impairment, but the Lord can change your condition. You can be just like His servant Moses who, even though he stuttered, became one of God's most important servants written about in the Bible."

Then the angel on the left spoke. "The Lord wants to help you become an eloquent speaker and wants to use you as a living witness so that others who have learning disabilities will be able to see the Spirit of God that is in you, so that, not only will they be delivered from their learning disabilities, but from their sins and any other obstacles the devil has set before them. The devil has told them they will never become anything in life and their future is limited."

I woke up from my dream feeling a peaceful Presence for which there are not enough words in the dictionary to describe. *What a difference between the message in last night's dream and the previous dreams about my imaginary friend,* I thought to myself.

The next scheduled school day, as I walked home from school down Hillman Street, I noticed a Christian counseling center called The Needle's Eye, which had two colorful signs posted in the window. One read "SMILE. GOD LOVES YOU," and the other said "YOU ARE SOMEBODY BECAUSE GOD DOES NOT MAKE JUNK."

As the days passed, I could not walk by that window without being drawn to look at those signs. Finally one day I entered the counseling center and was greeted by a very sweet lady named Irma Davis. "Hi, may I help you?" she asked.

I explained to her, "E-e-every d-d-day when I w-w-walk to s-s- school I n-n-notice the s-s-signs you have p-p-posted in your w-w- window. I-I-I c-c-can't s-s-seem to t-t-take m-m-my eyes o-o-off them."

Each day after school, in spite of all the chores and errands awaiting me, I took time to stop at the center before going home. After talking with Mrs. Davis several times, I was surprised that, although she had never met any of my family, she knew everything about me. As if someone had actually told her about me, she knew that I had a learning disability and even knew that my parents were divorced. She even seemed to sense how responsible I felt for their divorce. Talking with her was like being in the presence of a prophet of God.

Gradually, as my trust in her deepened, I shared my hurts and concerns and about my imaginary friend. One day I mustered up enough courage to tell her about my crush on a very popular girl at school whose parents held a high status in society. I explained to Mrs. Davis, "M-m-my im-m-maginary fr-fr-friend t-t-told m-m-me t-t-to approach th-th-this young l-l-lady and ask h-h-her if I-I-I c-c- could c-c-carry her b-b-books and w-w-walk her h-h-home."

The young lady had glared at me. "You are not good enough, nor are you smart enough to carry MY books home! Anyway, I don't want anybody to see me walking home with a DUMB-BELL!"

Mrs. Davis looked as if she could cry. "Sit down, Lonnie," she said and handed me a glass of iced tea. As I settled into the chair beside her desk, she began, "I want to tell you about the greatest love story ever written." She opened the Holy Bible. "Lonnie, I would like to read to you from Isaiah 53:1-10. Listen carefully.

"'Who hath believed our report? and to whom is the arm of the Lord revealed? For he shall grow up before him as a tender plant, and as a root out of a dry ground: he hath no form nor comeliness; and when we shall see him, there is no beauty that we should desire him. He is despised and rejected of men; a man of sorrows, and acquainted with grief: and we hid as it were our faces from him; he was despised, and we esteemed him not. Surely he hath borne our griefs, and carried our sorrows: yet we did esteem him stricken, smitten of God, and afflicted. But he was wounded for our transgressions, he was bruised for our iniquities: the chastisement of our peace was upon him; and with his stripes we are healed. All we like sheep have gone astray; we have turned every one to his own way; and the Lord hath laid on him the iniquity of us all. He was oppressed, and he was afflicted, yet he opened not his mouth: he is brought as a lamb to the slaughter, and as a sheep before her shearers is dumb, so he openeth not his mouth. He was taken from prison and from judgment: and who shall declare his generation? for he was cut off out of the land of the living: for the transgression of my people was he stricken. And he made his grave with the wicked, and with the rich in his death; because he had done no violence, neither was any deceit in his mouth. Yet it pleased the Lord to bruise him; he hath put him to grief: when thou shalt make his soul an offering for sin, he shall see his seed, he shall prolong his days, and the pleasure of the Lord shall prosper in his hand.'"

Mrs. Davis paused and looked into my eyes. Touched by those sacred words, I was speechless. Unable to read, I'd had to rely only on the portions of scripture I'd heard read on Sunday mornings in church. I could not recall ever having heard what Mrs. Davis had just read.

She explained to me in a soft compassionate voice, "Lonnie, the Lord Jesus Christ was rejected, stoned, spat upon, talked about. He did not have fancy clothes to wear and was not well-liked. Jesus Christ was not a rich person. Just as you have experienced people laughing about your clothing, Jesus Christ experienced being laughed at and mocked."

"Th-th-then the L-l-lord G-g-god H-h-hims-s-self w-w-went through the s-s-same h-h-hurts th-th-that I h-h-have!"

Mrs. Davis nodded and smiled. "Listen to John 3:1-21," she continued, leafing through the pages of the Bible toward the back of the book.

"'There was a man of the Pharisees, named Nicodemus, a ruler of the Jews: The same came to Jesus by night, and said unto him, Rabbi, we know that thou art a teacher come from God: for no man can do these miracles that thou doest, except God be with him. Jesus answered and said unto him, Verily, verily, I say unto thee, Except a man be born again, he cannot see the kingdom of God. Nicodemus saith unto him, How can a man be born when he is old? Can he enter the second time into his mother's womb, and be born? Jesus answered, Verily, verily, I say unto thee, Except a man be born of water and of the Spirit, he cannot enter into the kingdom of God. That which is born of the flesh is flesh; and that which is born of the Spirit is spirit. Marvel not that I said unto thee, Ye must be born again. The wind bloweth where it listeth, and thou hearest the sound thereof, but canst not tell whence it cometh, and whither it goeth: so is every one that is born of the Spirit. Nicodemus answered and said unto him, How can these things be? Jesus answered and said unto him, Art thou a master of Israel, and knowest not these things? Verily, verily, I say unto thee, We speak that we do know, and testify that we have seen; and ye receive not our witness. If I have told you earthly things, and ye believe not, how shall ye believe, if I tell you of heavenly things? And no

man hath ascended up to heaven, but he that came
down from heaven, even the Son of man which is in
heaven. And as Moses lifted up the serpent in the
wilderness, even so must the Son of man be lifted up:
That whosoever believeth in him should not perish, but
have eternal life. For God so loved the world, that he gave
his only begotten Son, that whosoever believeth in him
should not perish, but have everlasting life. For God sent
not his Son into the world to condemn the world; but that
the world through him might be saved. He that believeth
on him is not condemned: but he that believeth not is
condemned already, because he hath not believed in the
name of the only begotten Son of God. And this is the
condemnation, that light is come into the world, and
men loved darkness rather than light, because their
deeds were evil. For every one that doeth evil hateth the
light, neither cometh to the light, lest his deeds should
be reproved. But he that doeth truth cometh to the light,
that his deeds may be made manifest, that they are
wrought in God.'"

She paused again to allow the message of the Holy Word to
sink into my mind, then explained, "Lonnie, the world has
always been so filled with wickedness and sin, with hate and the
lack of love and compassion for our fellow man, that the Lord
Jesus Christ knew the only way He could save a dying world
from sin would be for Himself, being God, to become flesh. Even
though He was rejected by men, talked about and cursed—
hated by the world—He never ceased to be God. He never
stopped caring for those who hated Him and talked about Him."
    "I-I-I c-c-can h-h-hardly b-b-believe that G-g-god H-h-
hims-s- self was r-r-rej-j-jected and t-t-talked ab-b-bout, s-s-
spat on, st- st-stoned, y-y-yet bec-c-came a-a-a l-l-living s-s-
sacrif-f-fice in order t-t-to s-s-save a d-d-dying w-w-world from
s-s-sin!"
    "Lonnie, the Lord understands your hurts, and cares about
your problems, and He loves you in spite of your shortcomings
and learning disabilities. The devil knows that and will do
everything he can to keep you from knowing about the love of
God. He will tell you to do bad things such as you have been

doing to keep you in sin and guilt." *The devil will tell me to do bad things?* Something seemed to snap within my mind and my chest. *Could my imaginary friend be the devil in disguise?* Before I had time to think through this new truth, Mrs. Davis continued, "If you will just put the Lord Jesus Christ first in your life, Lonnie, He will give you power to overcome the evil forces of hell. The Lord will take you like a piece of clay, and lovingly mold and shape you into what He would have you to be. You will receive a new mind and will be able to understand and comprehend your learning materials from school." I drank in her every word.

"Lonnie, I believe the Lord wants to use you to be a light on a hill for those who have learning disabilities and are faced with the problems of life. Like a ship that is lost at sea and is guided by the lighthouse, they will be able to see His Light in you, Lonnie. Even though you have a speech impairment, the Lord wants to make you an eloquent speaker to be a witness— to tell people who have problems like yours, 'You are not an exception. With man this is impossible, but with the Lord all things are possible if you will just ask the Lord to come into your life.'"

My dream about the two angels! I thought. *Mrs. Davis is telling me the same thing the angels were saying!* I knew the Lord had spoken to Mrs. Davis because I had told no one about that dream. Immediately I fell to my knees. "L-l-lord J-j-jesus Ch-ch-christ," I prayed, "c- c-come int-t-to m-m-my l-l-life. F-f-forg-g-give m-m-me f-f-for the s-s-sins I-I-I've com-m-mitted. R-r-rem-m-make m-m-my m-m-mind. M-m- mold m-m-me and sh-sh-shape m-m-me into wh-wh-what You would h-h-have m-m-me to b-b-be."

Each day I spent time at The Needle's Eye, running errands, passing out Bibles, stocking shelves with literature, or helping unload truckloads of food and clothing donated to the center to be distributed to those in need.

For the first time in my life I felt peace in my soul. All the guilt and shame, the feeling of being dirty and inferior were gone. I had been cleansed from all my sins. The old Lonnie had passed away. I had become a totally new and different person! Through Jesus Christ I had become a somebody!

Through reading and hearing the Word of God that inner peace grew. Romans 3:23, "All have sinned and come short of the glory of God," assured me that I wasn't the worst person in the world, nor was I the only one who had ever done bad things. Knowing this made it easier for me to acknowledge every sin I had ever committed and ask for forgiveness. I asked Mrs. Davis, "What makes me feel like I'm a new person? I feel so clean, like I will never again be the same."

"Lonnie, you've been born again."

For the first time, I knew I was somebody in the Lord. I was delivered from the nightmares of my imaginary friend. I had the full understanding that the devil had been trying to take control of my mind and soul. The devil knew that the Lord had a special purpose for my life.

In follow-up visits Mrs. Davis taught me to pray so that any satanic spirit and that dumb spirit was bound in the name of Jesus and sent back to the lake of fire.

Chapter 10
On to Junior High

A new power began to influence my mind. My grades improved because I could understand more of what my teachers were saying.

Mrs. Davis at The Needle's Eye regularly reminded me, "Lonnie, whenever you run into a problem at school, don't become disturbed. Just remember the Bible verse we taught you, 'I can do all things through Christ who strengthens me'" (Philippians 4:13).

That's what I held on to every day. I learned to take time to pray before completing every assignment and taking every test.

"Lord, you've got me," I would pray. "Use my mind. Help me to understand and to remember."

I noticed that the attitudes of my teachers towards me had changed. Often they would ask, "Lonnie, is there anything you're having a problem with? Stop in after class and I'll be happy to help you out."

My steady progress in grade school, as a result of the various Motivation and LAMPS classes, enabled me to enter my first year in Princeton Junior High with a new confidence. No longer was I intimidated by the knowledge that I had a learning disability.

My classmates no longer ridiculed and harassed, except occasionally in study hall. "Hey, Lonnie," they would ask, "what's that you're readin'?"

"Th-th-the B-b-bible," I would respond. Even though I had overcome my reading disability through prayer, I continued to be plagued with severe stuttering.

They would chuckle and comment to one another, "Ol' Lonnie's got his nose in his Bible again!" But they gave me no problems.

Their teasing about my reading the Bible didn't bother me, because whenever they had problems they came to me during study hall and asked, "Hey, Lonnie, what's the Bible have to say about this?" Then they would tell me about the trouble they were having with their school work or their family, etc.

From the moment I accepted the Lord into my life, the old Lonnie was cast away. Although I remained a loner, I had begun a completely new way of life.

Unlike elementary school, my first year in junior high was very exciting. In the elementary grades the teachers had told me everything I had to do and, in many cases, had helped me with my homework assignments. As a junior high student, I found that, instead of my teachers checking on me all the time, I had to assume more responsibility for completing my assignments and preparing for exams. Although the teachers were willing to help, I had to take the initiative to ask.

Another thing I liked about junior high school was the fact that, with the help of a counselor, I could select some of the classes I would take.

In a meeting with my mother, my teachers recommended that, even though I had made great progress in reading and writing, it might be wise for me to continue with the special classes on the junior high level, since I might still have some problems with grammar or spelling.

I was not really upset that I would have to attend these classes, because I learned that Mr. Rozzi and his assistant Miss Thelma Barnes had transferred to junior high. For the first time in my life I looked forward to going to school.

During my first day in class with Mr. Rozzi, he began to work with me to overcome my speech impairment. The class was reading a short play. Each of the ten students had a small part about a paragraph long. After class and during study times, Mr. Rozzi had me read my assigned paragraph over again and again, so I could become confident enough to pronounce every word correctly without stuttering.

About two weeks passed. During reading class Mr. Rozzi pointed to me and said, "Okay, Lonnie, it's your turn to read."

Deep inside I was afraid because I was sure my speech impairment would cause me to stumble over the verbs and nouns. Painful memories of the laughter in elementary school rang in my mind. But something happened to me in that classroom. As I looked down at the paragraph I was supposed to read, the Spirit of God came upon me and told me, "Lonnie, open up your mouth and I will speak through you. I will be with you and will guide each word you speak. You will speak eloquently."

I began to read the paragraph and felt like God was actually speaking through me. There was no way I could have recited that paragraph like I did. The entire class applauded!

When their applause had faded somewhat, Mr. Rozzi interrupted with an upraised hand and said, "Lonnie, I would like to see you immediately outside the classroom."

Abruptly my elation faded. *Now what have I done wrong?* I asked myself. My heart quivered as I followed my favorite teacher out the door and into the hallway. "Wait right here," he instructed and hurried down the corridor. As I waited I began to worry more. *What HAD I done wrong?* Mr. Rozzi returned with Mr. Jim Thorpe who was in charge of all the public speaking classes. Why is he bringing Mr. Thorpe to talk to me? I wondered, my hands trembling. Only honor students are accepted into his class.

As the two teachers approached the spot to which I was glued just outside the classroom door, Mr. Rozzi smiled. "Jim, I want you to listen to this young man read." He hurried back into the room and returned with a copy of the same paragraph I had read during the class play.

In spite of my nervousness, I heard God say to me, "Lonnie, I am with you. Just open up your mouth and I will give you the ability to read that paragraph effectively." I did exactly what God told me to do.

I read without stumbling over a single word. Both Mr. Rozzi

and Mr. Thorpe frowned in disbelief, then smiled at one another. As if I were not present, they huddled together and began to talk. All I heard was Mr. Thorpe saying, "We can use him in public speaking." With enthusiasm Mr. Rozzi nodded in agreement, opened the classroom door and motioned for me to enter. He shut the door after me and continued to talk with Mr. Thorpe.

My head swirled. What was happening to me? Was I getting into something that would be over my head? I couldn't decide whether my continued trembling was from excitement or fear. My classmates stared in silence as I walked to my seat. They too wondered what I had done to create such a stir.

"What happened, Lonnie?" someone asked. "What's wrong?" I could only shrug my shoulders. All I knew was that the Lord had told me to open up my mouth and he would speak through me.

After class was over that day, Mr. Rozzi called me aside and told me, "Lonnie, I want to enter you into a public speaking contest."

I said to myself, *There's no way I could stand up in front of people and compete against top speakers from other schools!* Trembling, I repeated my thoughts to him. "Mr. Rozzi, there's no way I could do that. You know I have a very bad speech impairment. I stutter over my words. I can't do anything like that."

"Lonnie, there was something about the way you read that paragraph— it was like someone was speaking through you. Listen to yourself. You're not stuttering any more!" My eyes filled with tears of gratitude to God. A miracle had taken place in my life!

Mr. Rozzi encouraged me to consent to competing against various schools in the city of Youngstown and surrounding areas. He told me, "Lonnie, I'll write the speech for you." I was slightly relieved, knowing he understood that I was not capable of writing a speech which would be acceptable to a panel of judges. The speech he wrote for me was entitled, "Tomorrow's Promise: What I Hope Tomorrow's Promise Will Bring."

Over a series of days and weeks he spent hours after school coaching me on how to get up in front of people and which way to turn and move my hands. From time to time Mr. Thorpe would slip into the classroom to listen and offer suggestions for improvement.

One day Mr. Rozzi told me, "Lonnie, just go on over to Mr. Thorpe's class instead of staying in here today."

The big day finally came. As I arrived at the contest sponsored by the Rotary Club, representing the city of Youngstown, I found I would be competing against eloquent speakers from wealthy families. I listened to their speeches and became more and more nervous. *No way can I do this!* I thought to myself. I trembled from head to foot.

South High Sophomore Gets Honor

Lonnie Clinkscale, a sophomore at South High School, won the annual oratorical contest of the Buckeye Elks Lodge Sunday at the Elks Youth Development Center on North Avenue.

The 17-year-old spoke on "Abraham Lincoln and the U.S. Constitution." He is a son of Mr. and Mrs. Eddie Clinkscale, 1014 Overland Ave.

He will compete in the district contest of the Elks Northern District Council of Ohio at the Youth Development Center at 7 p.m. Saturday, April 15. The winner in that event will compete in the state contest in June at the Ramada Inn, in conjunction with the convention of the Ohio Association Elks.

Finishing in the top four were Shelley Watson, 17, a senior at Cardinal Mooney High, second; Jewel Ann Wooten, 15, a sophomore at East High, third; and Bertrand Gray, 14, an eighth grader at West Junior High.

Judges were Joseph Curry, international sales representative for Commercial Shearing Inc.; Mrs. Sarah Brown Clark, English professor at Youngstown State University; and Raymond Brown, principal of Rayen School.

The contest chairman was William Anderson. Elizabeth Pennington was cochairman. Mizell Stewart is Buckeye Elks exalted ruler and president of the state association.

SPEECH WINNER — Lonnie Clinkscale, winner of the Buckeye Elks' annual oratorical contest, receives his award from William Anderson, contest chairman.

Chapter 11
Victories and Break-
throughs

The time came for me to give my speech before the panel of judges at The Rotary Club Area Competition held in a nearby community. I was in such a dream world I can't even remember where it was held or how I got there, but the rows and rows of students who filled the auditorium are a vivid memory. As I approached the podium, the Lord spoke to me. "Lonnie, I will be with you to the end of the world. Remember what I told you the day you accepted Me into your life? I WILL make you an eloquent speaker. All you need to do is open your mouth and have faith in Me. If I could speak to a whole nation through Moses who had a speech impairment, I can use you. All I want you to do is have faith in Me. Believe that I will speak through you."

As I stood in front of the hundreds of people who were there, I quickly scanned the audience to locate Mr. Rozzi who was to signal when I was to raise or lower my voice. I began to read the speech Mr. Rozzi had prepared for me. "As I think of the promises of tomorrow, I am very much concerned about the leadership of this great nation..." The power of God took complete control of my mouth and my voice. "I shall hope that our president would not only think of himself, but would also think of our nation as a whole before concerning himself with the needs of other nations.

"Please don't misunderstand me. I don't mean to sound selfish. But I believe that we must first concern ourselves with the needs of the people in our nation before helping those abroad. I shall hope that tomorrow's promise does not bring such things as wars and rumors of wars. I shall hope that our president would make every effort to maintain peace throughout America as well as the rest of the world.

"I hope that tomorrow's promise will bring no such thing as hunger throughout the world, when children die as a result of lack of food and their parents resort to some type of crime in order to support their family. I shall hope that tomorrow's promise will bring no such thing as drugs which have polluted the minds of our youth. It has ripped many families apart and resulted in the destruction of the family unit.

"I shall also hope that our nation would be free from pollution. The cause of the deterioration of our environment in many cases has resulted in our animals becoming an endangered species because their environment and habitat has been destroyed with pollution and toxic chemicals.

"I shall also hope that tomorrow's promise shall have a more humane way of taking care of our elderly without placing them in nursing homes. I shall also hope that in tomorrow's promise our elderly would be able to walk the streets and to live in their homes without the fear of being mugged or robbed."

By this time I couldn't even hear what I was saying. Before I knew it, I was reading the last line on the last page laying on the podium before me. "What is your promise for tomorrow? Will it be for a better and safer tomorrow? Will it be for peaceful government throughout the world? I hope so, because only you can bring about the promise of tomorrow."

The ordeal was over! Relieved, I wondered how my delivery had been received. Looking over the podium, my eyes nervously scanned the audience. Everyone was standing and clapping their hands. *A standing ovation! I can't believe it!* I turned toward the twenty-nine other contestants. To my surprise they, too, were applauding. I sensed they were also shocked at my performance.

Trying to remain calm, I strained to locate Mr. Rozzi's familiar face in the crowd. I felt my chest would burst when I saw that he and many of the dignitaries who were present had also risen to their feet and were applauding vigorously. For the first time in my life I received a golden trophy, but felt uncomfortable accepting the honor, because I knew full well that my victory had come about only because God had spoken through me. He deserved the honors.

Winning that contest was a turning point in my life. I had God AND self-esteem. A light bulb clicked on in my head. "Hey, Lonnie Clinkscale, you're not so dumb after all! Now that you have God in your life, you're no longer a dummy!"

The Lord had challenged, "Try Me." And because I stepped out in faith and opened up my mouth, God used me.

The Youngstown Vindicator announced that Lonnie Clinkscale had taken first place representing Youngstown schools and would be competing in district competition, which I did. Out of thirty people I placed second in the district. All of my teachers were shocked when they heard that I, the slowest guy in elementary school, the guy who couldn't speak and couldn't even spell his first name and did not know how to add two plus two, had competed against honor students and won. It was God. It was the Lord moving in my life. Again and again He had reassured me, "Even though the odds have been against you in your learning disabilities, with Me in your life... With men it is impossible but with God all things are possible."

The next school day, Mr. Thorpe called me into his class-room. As I entered the room and closed the door behind me, Mr. Thorpe, upset because none of his honor students had ever placed in a similar contest, held out his hand toward me and announced to the class, "Here we have a young man who has had a learning disability and a speech impairment all through his years of school. He placed second in the competition. You are honor students and not one of you placed. For the first time, thanks to Lonnie, we beat our greatest rival." The tone of his voice indicated he was both puzzled and pleased. Then he told the class, "And I want each of you to take notes while he talks."

Some of my other teachers requested, "Recite your winning speech for the class, Lonnie." I could have burst with pride and with gratitude to God.

The trophy I received was placed in the school's trophy case and left there until I graduated. Now it is in my home as a reminder of my victory over my inability to study and of my breakthrough, the realization that through the power of God I have become a somebody.

"Congratulations, Lonnie," one of my classmates told me after class as we passed in the hallway.

"Yeh," another chimed in, then nodded in my direction. "He's real heavy."

"He's neat all right," someone else added. "A smart kid! How'd you do that, Lonnie?"

"It was God," I explained to them, nodding toward the Bible on top of the pile of books I carried in my arm. "The Lord made me what I am today. He's the one who gets credit."

They chuckled. "He's a Jesus freak all right!" said one of the fellows in a gentle manner. I loved it! I had no further problems getting along with the kids in school. Times had changed!

In my second year at Princeton Junior High, I placed first in the Rotary contest. Every time I competed against the various schools in the city and in the district, the Lord blessed me to take first place and write-ups were placed in the newspapers. Some of those articles are included in this book.

With pride my mother accompanied me to the district contests. Once while I was visiting my father, I mustered up enough courage to ask him, "Would you like to hear the speech I'll be giving on Saturday when I represent the district?"

"Why, yes, I guess so," he answered. He sat down in his favorite chair. "Go ahead, Lonnie, let's hear it."

After I had finished, he smiled and said, "Lonnie, I like that. Yes, I like that." Then he looked away with a wistful expression on his face. "I've always wished I could get up in front of people and speak." He gave me some pointers for improvement. I was thrilled.

Both of my parents went with me to one of the major contests. It was the first time they had gone anywhere together for months! On our way home, my father confessed, "I know I haven't taken the time to come to your competitions to hear you speak, Lonnie, but I see in you a lot of things that remind me of myself and my own struggles throughout life." *He saw himself in me? I was doing something right in my father's eyes?* For a change he could be proud of his son! He continued, "Lonnie, I no longer have to worry about you. I know you can take care of yourself. I regret that I don't call you very often to see how you are doing, but I *know* you're going to be okay from now on."

I explained, "Daddy, it's not Lonnie that's taking care of Lonnie, it's God who has kept me out of trouble."

When we arrived at home, my younger sisters ran out of the house to meet us. "Daddy! Mommy! How did Lonnie do? Did he get first place?"

"He took first place!" my father informed them. They shouted and clapped with joy.

As my mother opened the door of the car, my father held his hand over the back of the driver's seat to stop me from getting out. "Son, stay in the car. I want to take you out to dinner. You can order anything you want." I felt good!

When we were nearly finished eating, I noticed the expression on my father's face softened. "Lonnie," he said in the most gentle tone of voice I had ever heard him use, "I want to apologize for spending so little time with you as you were growing up. Your mother and I were married and began our family when we were very young, so I never had a chance to enjoy life. I have never been the father I wanted to be. I guess I never knew how to relate to a family." Then he brightened, as if a great idea had just come to him. "Lonnie, I don't have much money, but I want to take you to the store. I want you to buy anything you want." I thought I must be dreaming!

The drive to the department store was made brief by our light chatter and relaxed laughter. The moment we entered the clothing department, I spotted a beautiful gray silk shirt. I could not take my eyes off it. I had always admired silk.

My father repeated, "Lonnie, buy anything you want. I know I can't make up for the years that have passed. I can't go back into history and make it different. But I want to show you that Daddy really does love you." I lifted the hanger off the rack to examine the shirt more closely. A picture of The Thinker was imprinted on the back. *This is what I want,* I said to myself. *But can Dad afford it?* I fingered the price tag and was alarmed to see that it said "$30.00."

"Dad, I want this shirt," I told him hesitantly, doubting that he could afford to buy it.

My father pulled his wallet from his back pants pocket and counted the money in it. Then he reached deep into his other pocket, pulled out some change and counted it. Once again, he dug into the pocket, pulled out change and counted. He looked at me and smiled.

"Son, if that's what you want, then Daddy will buy it for you." I could tell it took his last dime to get me the shirt. He wrapped his arms around me and said, "Son, I really love you." I had never heard my father say that before. Inside I had a deep warm feeling that convinced me he was truly sorry that he couldn't go back and make things right. His love was real. All the misconceptions I'd felt about him, all my fear of him melted away and I fully understood why he had not been the father I had always hoped he could be. I felt his frustrations, his inability to be the kind of person he had always wanted to be.

In recent years, the Lord has begun a great work of inner healing in my father and in his relationships with his children. He spends more time with us now than he did in all our growing up years.

Chapter 12
From Dummy to Scholar

Not only was I doing well in public speaking, but the Lord also blessed me to be able to accomplish even more by faith. As a result of His gentle manner of teaching, I felt that He had taken my whole brain in the palm of His hand and was remolding and reshaping it as if it were a piece of clay. I continued to place first in public speaking competitions. For the first time in my life I excelled in my studies, earning A's and B's. It was miraculous how, as I stepped out in faith, God worked through me, enabling me to be successful.

The Lord had given me the key for doing well in my school work. "Lonnie, in order for you to be a success and do well in your tests and studies, every day when you go to class, before you pick up your books, take time to pray. Always pause long enough to ask Me to guide you and to shape your mind, to give you clear understanding so you will be able to comprehend and remember everything you need to know."

Every time I opened my books I prayed, "Lord, take control of my mind. Give me the wisdom and knowledge I need to study the materials I am about to read. Lord, give me a clear understanding of what my teachers will be saying."

Each day after I went home from school, I took time out

before doing my homework to ask the Lord, "Guide me, shape my mind, so I will be able to remember everything that was taught in class today in order for me to complete my homework assignments." The Lord Jesus Christ taught me how to study and how to do my homework.

Not only did the Lord help me with my school work, He also provided me with a sufficient income to support my mother and me. I often recall with gratitude the many hours I spent cutting lawns and running errands for my customers.

One Saturday morning Mr. Marinelli, an OWE teacher at South High School, saw me cutting a neighborhood lawn with a lawn-mower that was beyond repair. (OWE, Opportunity Work Experience, is an organization which helps students who are determined to excel in life.) Mr. Marinelli pulled his automobile to the curb and motioned for me to stop mowing.

I walked to his parked car and through the open window he said, "Young man, I have heard a lot of good things about you. I understand you will be entering the tenth grade this fall and that in junior high you made great progress with your speaking ability. I was pleased to learn about the fine job you have done representing Princeton Jr. High in speaking competition."

I could hardly believe what I was hearing. Most of my life I had heard only negative things about myself. This man was saying he was impressed with me and saw something special in me! I thanked him and he continued, "It looks like that lawn-mower you're using is unsafe. I want to help you get a better one." I thought I must be dreaming!

The following week Mr. Marinelli talked with my mother and received her permission to buy me a new lawn mower. The next day he took me to Sears and Roebuck. We walked to the Lawn and Garden department where a middle-aged clerk asked, "May I help you with something?"

Mr. Marinelli pulled out his credit card and told the sales representative, "As a matter of fact, you can. Give this young man the best lawn mower in the store."

Because I believed the Lord had become my Father, I felt He was showing me His love and concern through Mr. Marinelli. Whatever I needed He had begun to provide through others.

Soon after I began to attend South High School I frequently

heard my teachers refer to Career Day and learned that each year one school day was set aside to help the students decide what kind of vocation they were most suited for and most interested in. On the first Career Day I had opportunity to participate in after entering high school, my teacher asked me, "Lonnie, what are your plans?"

"I would like to go to college."

She stared at me as if she had seen a ghost and replied, "Lonnie, having looked at your elementary school records, I feel you are not college material. I suggest that you look into joining the Army. You would make a good foot soldier."

For a moment I was discouraged, but then I realized my teacher was speaking about the old Lonnie. I was a new person in God. Regardless of what that teacher had said, I knew I must believe without a shadow of a doubt that my God was a God who could not and would not lie. While I was composing myself to continue on with my participation in Career Day, the Lord spoke to me, "You can do all things through Christ that strengthens you. (Philippians 4:13) You must learn to walk by faith." I regained my confidence in the Lord. Whenever I become discouraged I remember that Scripture.

Not long after I entered my first year at South High School, I was asked to represent the school in public speaking competitions and did very well competing against various schools throughout the state of Ohio. The Lord had moved so powerfully in my life that, not only did I compete against schools, but I was called upon to speak at numerous community functions and to represent several community organizations in public speaking competitions.

Mr. Marinelli asked me to speak at an OWE banquet to which many top businessmen and company representatives were invited. These guests supported the OWE program with financing and job opportunities for students.

Some of the churches throughout the state of Ohio invited me to give my testimony about how the Lord had transformed into a somebody a boy everyone thought would always be a nobody. People became excited when they heard how the power of the Lord had helped me after I had permitted Him to take complete control over my mind and my tongue, how He had molded into a good student and public speaker someone who had not even been able to spell the word "dog" or add 2+2 and could not read a complete sentence without stumbling over the words.

At those speaking engagements I was often asked, "Lonnie, are you the exception?" I always explained, "I believe that with God there are no exceptions. When you trust God with your life, regardless of the severity of your learning disability, He will bring you through." Every promise the Lord has made to me He has kept.

During my senior year in high school, Mr. Rozzi and Mr. Marinelli urged me to run for class president and for president of the OWE class. I was elected for OWE president and lost the class president election by only 20 votes. This was very encouraging for me because I realized the Lord had created in me a new person who received favor among the students, even though I had been talked about and laughed at in elementary school. Most important of all, I had favor with the Lord.

Chapter 13
Lonnie Clinkscale,
High School Graduate

Because I had come to the point where I needed a more substantial income than my meager earnings from cutting lawns and washing walls, I decided to talk with Mr. Marinelli. Part of his responsibility as OWE coordinator was to find jobs so students could work for half a day and attend school the other half.

A few days after our talk, Mr. Marinelli sent a message to my final class for the day and asked that I come to his office before leaving school. It was difficult for me to concentrate on my studies throughout the rest of the class period, because I was anxious to find out what he wanted.

As I opened the door to his office, Mr. Marinelli looked up and smiled. I was certain I was about to hear good news. "I have the ideal job for you, Lonnie," he said as I stood before his desk. "You'll be working in a hospital. Can you go there with me now?" I assured him I could.

He drove me to St. Elizabeth's Medical Center in his white Oldsmobile and introduced me to John Smith, the housekeeping supervisor. Mr. Smith informed me that I could have a job cleaning patients' carts, wheelchairs and rest rooms.

Thrilled with the prospect of a *real* job, I immediately accepted and became known as the best commode cleaner in the hospital. I was considered by my fellow employees to be "The Commode Specialist." If a patient had a mishap or there was a tough stain that no one else could remove, I was the one who was paged to do the job.

I was very proud of my job, because I was earning $2.85 an hour and learning what it meant to be a dependable employee. I gave the Lord 10 percent of my gross pay and continued to give my mother half of my wages.

My work hours were from 5:00 to 9:00 p.m. I attended school from 8:00 a.m. to 2:00 p.m. and at 3:30 began to walk to the north side of town in order to be at work on time. Once I completed my daily job I walked back to my home on the south side of town.

As winter approached I had a difficult time walking back and forth to work, so my mother decided to buy a car—not a very good one, but the best she could afford. Although she had no driver's license, she faithfully chauffeured me home from work each day.

I never neglected to ask the Lord to guide and protect mother and me as we traveled back and forth on the dangerous city highways. At times that automobile was on the sidewalk more than it was on the road! Yet the Lord protected us and the other drivers on the streets. As soon as we could afford to do so, my mother and I purchased a more dependable car and received our driver's licences.

Because the Lord had blessed me to do well in school, Mr. Smith, my supervisor at the hospital, informed me, "Lonnie, since you have been able to keep your grades up while you've worked part time, when you graduate from high school I am going to employ you full time."

I thanked the Lord, realizing it was only through His love and guidance that I could have done so well. I vowed that I would not be a disappointment to Him.

I continued to be a very somber person and somewhat of a loner. Prior to graduation, I did not particpate in parties or even attend the prom. I just wanted to spend time with the Lord and continue to set a Godly example on my job.

The day of graduation was an exciting experience. Just before I marched down the aisle with my class, Mother hugged me. Although I was deeply disappointed that my father was not there, both my mother and I cried for joy. Even though the odds had been against me, the Lord brought me through to that special day of June 16, 1980.

I asked the Lord Jesus Christ to walk down the aisle with me to receive my diploma. Out of two hundred and fifty-five students who graduated from South High that day, I was in the top thirty, not bad for one who was told he would never graduate from high school and the only future he could look forward to was to join the Army since he was not college material!

After the graduation ceremony my mother suggested, "Lonnie, why don't we stop in at the Christian Counseling Center? After all, it was through Mrs. Davis the Lord convinced you that by trusting in Him you could succeed."

"That's a good idea!" I told her.

As we entered the counseling center I was greeted by the Christian counselors, a few of my teachers and some fellow students. They had planned a surprise graduation party for me. The inscription on the cake read: "You Are Somebody Because God Does Not Make Junk."

Tears of joy streamed down my cheeks, and love welled up in my heart for all those who had taken time out to help a slow learner realize he was somebody in God. Who would have ever thought that the slowest guy in school would finish in the top portion of his class?

The Lord has shown me over and over again that He loves me. And He loves you. I pray that you will learn to have faith in Him. The devil will try to discourage you, but if you believe God in spite of the odds, He will be faithful and help you through your difficulties.

About a year after graduation from high school I entered my mother's bedroom to check on her as I always did when I came home from work and was surprised to find her still awake. "Lonnie, you're getting older now and you can't always be with me. I think you should start looking for an apartment of your own, closer to the hospital. Since your father is moving to Loraine, why don't you rent his apartment?" It was in just the right location so I followed her advice.

I can make a dollar stretch longer than Main Street. Although I owned my own automobile, I continued to walk to work and to school. I just don't believe in wasting money.

Chapter 14
On to College

Through the Elks who sponsored some of my speaking performances, the Lord blessed me with the $2,000 Crandall Scholarship. This enabled me to enroll as a student at Youngstown State University. I also received a $500 scholarship from another organization. Naturally I selected speech communication as my major.

I was told I needed a minor, so I enrolled in a labor studies class under Dr. Russo, head of the Labor Studies Department. I found him to be a dedicated, dynamic teacher, but tough. He had the ability to make his students feel they were a part of every lecture he gave.

Dr. Russo stressed to his students, "You *will* learn in this class." In elementary school I had always made it a point to avoid strict or demanding courses. To my surprise, I considered trying to make it through Dr. Russo's class a challenge.

Often he repeated, "If you make it through this course, I guarantee that you will get a job in management."

After taking one of his classes, I was hooked and shifted to labor studies as my major, making communications my minor. Before I knew it, I had received a two-year degree in labor studies.

In order to graduate from Dr. Russo's class, each of his students was required to make up what he called a Bargaining Book, a huge, thick volume consisting of several hundred pages. I spent hours upon hours in the library researching labor disputes and laws, recording laws, definitions and examples of actual grievances between labor and management and how they had been settled. On numerous occasions Dr. Russo stated, "Once you complete this book I guarantee that you will be able to take this book to any employer and have a good chance of being hired in management."

Upon completing his course, I took my Bargaining Book to the Director of Environmental Services at the hospital and I believe that, with the help of the Lord, my Bargaining Book played a major part in my receiving several promotions.

To this day, when I see Dr. Russo, recollections of memorizing all the labor laws and other necessary information ring in my mind. I can still hear him lecturing. He was a dynamic teacher!

Returning to his classroom soon after I had completed the two- year course, I asked him, "Dr. Russo, do you teach any other programs?"

"No, Lonnie. You have completed your studies with me." I decided to finish the communications courses. Soon I will have a BA in speech communications, with emphasis in organizational communications.

When I talked with Dr. Russo recently, he told me, "Lonnie, after you complete your present courses, I would like to see you go to Indiana University in Bloomington to get a Master's Degree in Labor Relations. Don't worry about getting a job there or about the finances. I'm sure we can work with you to find you a job while you attend classes."

Through his teaching and my experiences at the hospital I have a great interest in the role of settling disputes between labor and management. I am looking forward to continuing my education in hospital administration.

Chapter 15
A New Interest

Some time after I had been employed by the hospital, I noticed that every day when I left 5 North to clean the main lobby, a very attractive young woman came to work through the Belmont Street entrance. The fact that she was always smiling and always carried a Bible in her hand attracted me to her.

For four years I watched her carefully and soon knew where she parked her car, which elevator she took, and that she worked on 5 South. I never saw her associate with any of the hospital employees I considered to be hard-living folk and never saw her come to work surrounded by a lot of guys. She had what I interpreted to be a holy manner.

When I cleaned on 5 South I often overheard patients comment about her kindness. She had the ability to cheer and comfort them. She was always courteous and spoke with respect, no matter whether she was talking with the patients, their visitors or other hospital employees.

Every day I could hardly wait for it to be time to speed-buff the lobby floors so I could see this young woman. One Saturday morning when she entered the Belmont Street lobby door I had to turn the buffer off so she could walk through. It was the perfect opportunity!

"Ma'am, I can't help but admire the way you carry your Bible to work every day," I said after I mustered up all the courage I could find.

She stopped and smiled. "Why, thank you."

"My name is Lonnie, what's yours?"

"Paulette."

"Where do you work?"

"Five South. I'm a ward clerk." I glanced at her Bible.

That same day, when I went up to 5 South to clean, Paulette was seated behind the desk at the nurses' station. "Where do you attend church?" I asked her, trying to appear casual.

"I go to an Apostolic holiness church."

"Which one?"

"Mt. Calvary."

Although I still attended the Baptist church on Sunday mornings, because of my new interest I began to go to evening services at Mt. Calvary. I found those services to be filled with dynamic preaching and teaching about how to live a holy life. The pastor, Bishop Wagner, was a very powerful and effective preacher. The people held to higher standards and morals than most folks. They didn't get involved in drinking, cursing, etc. I admired that.

When attending evening services at Mt. Calvary Pentecostal, I felt as if I were entering a new realm of Christian life, a training camp to prepare believers for ministry. God was speaking there. People were being healed. I found myself spending more and more time there.

Always I admired Paulette from a distance. She looked beautiful as she sang in the choir. I admired the way she carried herself. It was obvious that she loved the Lord.

One evening after the services I asked Paulette if I could come to her house to visit and she consented. I took her a bouquet of roses. We talked about nothing but the Scriptures. When the evening was nearly over I asked her, "May I take you out to dinner?"

"Yes, I'd like that," she said with a smile.

"How about tomorrow?" I dared to ask, thinking, This is too good to be true! She agreed.

The next day, after I went home from work, I went directly to the kitchen, sat down at the table and poured my heart out before the Lord.

"Lord, I really like this young lady and feel she is going to play an important part in my life. I am attracted to her because of her loyalty and dedication to You and to the people she cares for in the hospital. In fact, I believe this young lady is going to be my wife. I see in her all the qualities I have always wanted in a wife."

The Lord showed me through the Scriptures that as long as I kept myself before Him and did not indulge in fornication He would bless our relationship. "Lord, You know I'm a virgin," I told Him. "And I am *not* going to allow myself to indulge in the world, because I have learned that if I submit myself to You, You will bless me with the desires of my heart. At the same time You will bless me with what You desire for me."

The Lord continued to assure me that because of my unwavering faith in Him, and because I had made a decision not to indulge in the things of the world, He would bless me.

On Sweetest Day I sent Paulette flowers with a card signed "Paulette, With Love, Lonnie Clinkscale." When it was delivered to her house, Paulette's mother, Pauline, answered the ring of the door bell and received the bouquet. Glancing briefly at the card, she mistook them to be for her. Paulette, suspecting there had been a mistake, said, "Let me see that card." Her mother removed it from the flowers and handed it to her. "Why, this says Paulette, not Pauline. These are for me!"

From one of our conversations about food likes and dislikes, I learned that Paulette liked cherries. The next day, determined to please her, I bought her a whole grocery bag full of them.

She was just as interested in pleasing me. Before one of my visits at her home, she baked some delicious oatmeal cookies. I complimented her so highly that she had fresh oatmeal cookies every time I went to visit her.

Jokingly I always insisted that her father taste-test them before I arrived. Finally her father complained, "Paulette, I can't eat another oatmeal cookie. I feel like I've become Lonnie's guinea pig!"

As we dated we took seriously the counsel given at Mt. Calvary Church: When you are dating you shouldn't be at your girlfriend's house longer than a couple of hours because you could get involved in long periods of kissing which could lead to other things. We followed the plan of God according to Scripture until we were married.

Although people at work often teased me about Paulette, I could assure them with a clear conscience that our relationship was honorable and above reproach. "Oh, come on, Lonnie!" they would say. "You don't mean to tell us you don't...? There must be something wrong with you!"

An uncle scolded me for my morality. "You're a young man. Twenty-two years old. You should be ..." But I didn't believe that and the Lord blessed me for remaining obedient to His Word.

Early one evening when I stopped in to visit Paulette at her home, her parents told me to go into the kitchen where Paulette was putting the finishing touches on the evening meal.

"Lonnie, why don't you have something to eat with us?" she asked.

I told her, "No, I don't want to be the kind of person who has to eat every time I come over."

"Well, you'll be going home to eat alone. Since you're a bachelor you probably don't have much to cook in your apartment. Let me fix you something to eat."

Our eyes met. I told her, "Paulette, you are going to be my wife." Her eyes expressed surprise, but at the same time a smile came across her face. I knew she liked what I had said.

One evening while we were talking together in the living room of her parents' home, Paulette told me, "Lonnie, I had a dream in which the Lord showed me my husband. I believe that the man in my dream was you and that God has blessed me to marry you."

Paulette explained that in her dream she was kneeling at the foot of a huge mountain, asking the Lord to show her who her husband should be. The Lord interrupted her prayer by saying to her heart, "Hush! Listen!" When she became still, she heard a man praying on the other side of the mountain. The Lord instructed, "Listen to the man's prayer."

"Oh, Lord, who is to become my wife?" the voice spoke. As both people continued to pray, the mountain slowly disappeared until Paulette was able to see a young man on his knees. He looked up and stretched out his hands to meet Paulette's, but her hands were so small that they only covered the man's palms.

After she told me about her dream she requested, "Lonnie,

let me see your hands". A shiver ran from my shoulders to my knees as I held out my hands.

"Lonnie, they look exactly like the man's hands in my dream!" She laughed. "Okay, that settles it. Go home now." I told her good-bye and left with a song in my heart.

Our pastor does not believe that a couple should date more than a year or so before they marry. I agree with him one hundred per cent. After several months of dating we became engaged.

Paulette is very outgoing and loves to be with people, whereas I am more somber. I am uncomfortable in crowds and long to remain to myself. Often she gently teased me about always wearing a suit jacket and never smiling. Our differences sometimes resulted in problems.

Once when I was sick, Paulette came to clean my apartment on her way home from work. As she tidied up the kitchen, the silence that prevailed irritated her so much that she stood in the middle of the floor and screamed, "It's too quiet in here!"

"This woman is crazy!" I joked and burst out laughing, a rare thing for me to do.

"Lonnie! What's wrong with you? Are you okay?" Paulette said with delight. "I can't believe you actually laughed out loud!"

I explained to her that I could not recall seeing my parents laugh or have fun. I was always taught by my father that a man never cries or shows emotion. I often smiled, but rarely laughed out loud.

"I am going to keep trying my best," Paulette warned, "and you are going to learn to laugh."

Chapter 16
Wedding Plans

One day Paulette dropped by my apartment to visit me. Looking around the small rooms, she announced, "Lonnie, if we're going to get married, I'm not going to live in this apartment. It's too small."

"I agree," I told her. "It is too small." Because we wanted to spend our time away from work learning to become one in God, we decided not to take on the responsibility of owning a home and property right away. We rented an apartment in Austintown, a nearby community.

During the time we were making our plans to be married, the pastor at the Baptist church where I belonged moved away. I felt it was best for Paulette and me to be members of the same church, so I transferred my membership to Mt. Calvary. It was a strict church, but I felt we needed that in order to live as closely as possible to the way the Scriptures teach a family should live.

Our wedding was planned according to a dream Paulette had, in which the Lord instructed her that the color scheme was to be three shades of blue, the heavenly color. In her dream she saw a woman.

"I will send this lady to you," the Lord told her. "She is to bake your wedding cake."

Shortly after Paulette's dream, while she was walking down a hospital corridor, a woman she had never seen before passed her, hesitated, then turned back and asked, "Pardon me, are you married?"

"No," Paulette answered, a bit surprised at this stranger's question. "But I'm getting ready to be married."

The woman nodded knowingly, then announced, "The Lord told me I am to make your wedding cake. I want you to come over to my house and show me how you want it to be."

Certain that this was the woman in her dream, Paulette checked her work schedule and made arrangements to go to the lady's home.

"Do you have a design in your mind?" the woman asked. Paulette described the vision of a wedding cake which had been given to her in her dream. There was to be a total of seven cakes. Five were open Bibles all connected to one another, with Scriptures on the top. The Scriptures were printed on paper with charred edges, then laminated and inbedded in the icing on the top of each cake. The center cake was topped with my favorite Scripture on one page ("I can do all things through Christ which strengtheneth me." Philippians 4:13) and Paulette's on the other ("The blessing of the Lord, it maketh rich, and He addeth no sorrow with it." Proverbs 10:22).

Behind the cakes were several long taper candles, symbolizing the light of God in our marriage.

The lady was amazed. "I've never made a cake like that before!"

"Could I anoint your hands with oil," Palette asked, "so the work that comes forth will be pleasing to the Lord?"

"I'd welcome that!" she answered. Before Paulette left, they prayed together.

A few days later the lady called Paulette. "The Lord came to me in a dream and showed me how to make your cake. May I make one for another party to see how it will look?" Paulette told her she could. The white cakes with blue trimmings were beautiful.

We set our wedding date for August 22, 1982 but we soon learned that my cousin Lawrence and his fiancee had already planned to be married on that day. So we moved our date to

September 4th. After we had announced the date of our wedding, my cousin and his fiancee changed theirs to September 4th. We changed our date, for a third time, to September 25th.

When the announcement of Lawrence's wedding came out in the newpaper, many of our friends thought that Lawrence was my real name and that I had married my cousin's fiancee instead of waiting to marry Paulette. I had a lot of explaining to do!

We decided our first wedding invitation should be addressed to Jesus. We have it in our wedding album to this day.

Paulette was honored at four bridal showers. Two of them were planned around Scriptures. Favors for one were Bibles carved out of soap and for the other, bookmarks in the shape of a key with Proverbs 10:22 written on them.

I could not understand why I was never included in any of the showers. After all, I should have been as much a part of the joyous celebration as she. Each time I went with her, but the hostesses insisted that I leave and return when the party was over.

Shortly before we were married, I took Paulette to my family reunion which was so large it took up half the Mahoning County Country Club. When we entered the room filled with at least 500 people, Paullete stopped suddenly, her eyes wide with disbelief. "Lonnie, are all these people kin to you?" I told her they were. "I've never in my life seen such a large family!" I smiled and began to introduce her to the family members.

Many of the guests at our wedding were Paulette's former patients. Through her love for people she had formed many lasting friendships. Following our beautiful wedding ceremony, after Paulette and I walked down the aisle arm in arm and took our positions at the door, I pulled away from her.

Startled, she asked, "Lonnie, where are you going?"

"I can't stay here and greet all those people. I'll be too nervous."

"Stay, Lonnie. I'll be at your side... You *do* need lots of love! I will give you that love. And protection too."

Chapter 17
Parenting and Husbanding

A year or so after we were married, shortly before our first child was born, we purchased our first home. When Lonette was born prematurely on September 3, 1983, she weighed only two pounds, seven ounces. "Don't get your hopes up too high," our doctor warned us. "Since she was born after a six-month pregnancy, she may not make it. Plan on her remaining in the hospital for a long time."

At that time medical science concerning tiny babies was not as advanced as it is today, and we knew our baby's chances were slim. But Mt. Calvary had taught us faith. "You must have faith. You must believe God in spite of the odds." During every church service we heard testimonies about God bringing people we knew through the toughest of times. Some who had gone through experiences similar to ours came together to pray and fast for our little girl. The Lord moved.

The nurses at St. Elizabeth's went beyond the call of duty. If they had opportunity to respond to that comment, I know they would say, "Well, Lonnie, that's our job." But the care they gave to Lonette was fantastic. God worked through them to keep Lonette alive. If I had a million dollars I would donate some of it to that wing of the hospital.

Our daughter was expected to remain in intensive care for three months. Each day while we were at work at the hospital my wife and I went into the intensive care nursery and anointed our baby with oil and prayed.

There were discouraging moments. Soon after we were told she weighed only three pounds, the doctor called us in. "Lonette has lost weight. She has dropped to only two pounds." Only faith and prayer got us through. When she weighed four pounds we were allowed to hold her.

How the Lord blessed us! We were able to bring Lonette home two weeks earlier than estimated. She is now in second grade in school and is growing tall and graceful as a tree.

Five years later Crystal was born, also prematurely. "To save this baby is a light task for God," our pastor consoled us. "Have faith. If He could bring Lonette through, who only weighed two pounds, since Crystal weighs a little more, God can certainly bring her through."

Now, two years old Crystal eats anything she sees and is never still a moment. Although I would have liked to have had a son, this precious little girl has been a blessing to me. I call her my little Tiger because she acts just like a boy. I call both my girls Daddy's Little Angels. I am blessed to have my wife and two girls.

When it comes to parenting, I try to make sure I don't make the same mistake my father made. The love and attention I felt was lacking in my relationship with my father, I try to give to my daughters. I love to take Lonette bike riding and to the museums. Soon I am going to take her to a football game. Even though she won't understand what is going on, she will be with her father. I've already set that day aside.

Recently I told my wife, "Tomorrow, I want you to dress Lonette in her best dress. I'm going to put on my suit and she and I are going to go to the museum. From there we're going to go out to dinner. Just me and my daughter."

The best way to avoid making the same mistakes my father made is to deliberately plan to spend more time with my children.

I guess I have taken on some of my father's characteristics. If a bill is a day late, my father goes off track, so I know I am like him in that area. Frequently when I check to see if everything has been paid on time, my wife complains, "Lonnie, sometimes I feel you put me under a microscope."

I explain, "I like to have all our bills paid on time. No late bills!"

Paulette is more free-hearted than I. If she has five dollars and you need four and a half, she will give it to you.

When Paulette gets paid, that's her money, but I insist that even her bills must be paid on time. She helps out with family expenses, but the big load is my responsbility.

Many times when my father became angry he showed his anger. I have learned from observing him to get away from the situation and let off steam, even if I have to leave the house for a couple of hours and walk through the park kicking a pop can around. Then I come back, sit down and try to resolve the problem.

Even when I feel Paulette is in the wrong, I must apologize, because a man is the king of his house. His wife is the queen. The husband should never think that he has more power than his wife. Both must work together. But because a man is king over his household, he has to make sure everything runs smoothly, while the wife creates the spiritual atmosphere for the husband and the children.

Paulette and I had to come to the understanding that we are different. The Lord has dealt with both of us. Both Paulette's encouragement and the type of work I do have helped me to become a little more outgoing.

We've learned that neither of us can do God's transforming work for Him. Neither of us should try to change the other's makeup because what we think is best may prevent us from receiving God's blessings. The Lord has His own way of getting a person where he or she should be in His timing. The only thing we can do is stay before God in prayer so the Lord can answer the desires of our hearts.

Always let the love of the Lord bring about the necessary changes in your mate, because when He does it, it is done.

If you have a dispute with your spouse or a misunderstanding, it is important to always resolve it that same day. Paulette and I have learned through God that by coming together as soon as possible, we won't have to make the same mistakes our parents have made.

Although both of us are very busy persons, we spend as much time as possible together, sharing our love, giving the other as much attention as possible and talking over our situations and our plans.

We have learned to trust in God. That is what has sustained our marriage. Even though there are hard times, through the faith we have because of the teaching we have received at Mt. Calvary we are equipped to overcome life's obstacles.

Lonette, age 5 and her daddy

Chapter 18
Touch Somebody's Life

After Paulette and I were married, I continued to accept invitations to speak for community organizations and to give my testimony in area churches. Soon the Lord inspired me to write my own speeches dealing with social concerns and challenging people to live the Christian life. "It's time to go further in your speaking career," He advised and began to give me current topics to research at the library. He put related Scriptures in my mind.

The first speech the Lord inspired me to write was entitled "Time Is Running Out." In the middle of the night I awoke and wrote on the scratch pad I keep beside my bed, "Time, like running water, is running out. It can't be too soon, but soon it can be too late. Man has planned his own time, not realizing that sooner or later time is going to run out.

"Man sometimes forgets that in the beginning was the Word and the Word was God. When sin became unbearable to God, He gave His only Son to save us from our sins. We crucified Him; we did not believe His Word. So the Lord said He would come back like a thief in the night to take the ones who believe in Him to the Promised Land He has prepared for them. Man has forgotten the Word, therefore *time is surely running out!*"

Early the next morning I took my notes to the kitchen table and continued to write, noting that young people are overdosing on drugs, brother is turning against brother and father against son. Every day violence occurs and false preachers are exposed. Divorce is rampant and the quality of family life and education are deteriorating. "Where is your faith in God?" I wrote. "What does God want us to do? He is talking, but we're not listening. We're too concerned about immediate pleasure, not everlasting love and joy."

Not only is time running out for humans, I thought as I pondered this subject, *but also for plant and animal life. Many species are becoming extinct because we have polluted the waterways and burned the trees. Our foods are tainted with preservatives.* I put my thoughts on the paper, then concluded, "But we can make it if only we get closer to God. We must prepare ourselves for the coming of Jesus Christ. Many of you think you have plenty of time before Jesus returns, but, my friends, I'm telling you, time is running out like the sand in an hourglass. If you do not heed the signs of the times you will be left behind. Repent. Be baptized in the name of Jesus for the remission of sin."

I felt the Lord wanted me to write more speeches, so I began to pray, asking, "Lord, what else do you want me to write about?" He gave me more Scriptures and related topics. I researched them in the library and wrote speeches about them.

Several times Paulette would walk by as I wrote and ask, "Lonnie, what are you writing about today?" I would give her the title of the speech I was working on and the issue it addressed. "Why, I've written a poem about that!" she often said and I would introduce my topic with my wife's poem.

When I wrote a speech aimed at drug users, I wanted to shock them into realizing the consequences of continuing with their addiction. So I began my talk with Paulette's poem "I Want To Live."

This can't be true! It can't be me!
Let me out of this casket where I can be free!
I'm only seventeen—I can't be dead!
What is wrong with these people's heads?
I want to live! I want to see

What other mysteries this world offers me.
I shouldn't have used all of that dope,
But I couldn't help it—I just couldn't cope
With this life's mysteries and its pain.
I couldn't deal with going to church every day
Until I had gray hair and a cane.
I'm too young! I wanted the world to explore.
Raised in holiness, I wanted to see the other side.
I *had* to go through that door.

Mama, can't you hear me? Please don't cry!
Wait! Don't leave me here! I didn't die!
Why didn't I listen? I didn't take heed
To all the things Jesus said and did plead.
No matter how some backsliders left Christ,
I knew what was wrong and right.
Now I'm paying the price.
Everything you do in this life—
No matter how slick you are—
For your envy and strife you will pay.
God calls for holiness. This you must give.
Why wait 'til you die, then tell Him
"I want to live!"?

After I had written several speeches, I asked the Lord, "Why are You having me write all these speeches, Lord? What am I supposed to do with them?" I began to dream about speaking on the radio. Finally, one morning I looked through the listing of radio stations in the phone book and discovered WGFT, a Christian station. Immediately I dialed the number.

A man's voice responded to the ring of the phone. "Good morning. WGFT. Tim Capola, president, speaking."

The president! I thought. *I never cease to be surprised by God's timing.* "Good morning, Sir," I managed to reply. "This is Lonnie Clinkscale speaking. I've been led by the Lord to write several speeches which address current issues of today's society from a Christian perspective. Would you have any available air time for me to present them to the public?"

"Could you bring me copies or recordings of some of your work so I can preview them?"

"Why, yes, sir," I answered. "How soon can you see me?"

"How about tomorrow afternoon?"

"I'll be there! ...And thank you, Mr. Capola!"

Nervous and excited, I went to the radio station that Saturday afternoon while Paulette was at work and handed Mr. Capola cassettes of some of the speeches I had already given. He promised to listen to them right away. "Can you come in on Monday and meet with me?" he asked.

"Yes, sir. Is it all right if my wife Paulette comes with me?"

"Of course."

Lonnie Clinkscale, I thought on my way home, *the boy who couldn't read, couldn't think, couldn't remember, may have a radio program. Only You, Lord, could work a miracle like that!* I could hardly wait until Paulette came home from work to tell her the good news.

On Monday Paulette accompanied me to the radio station. The receptionist looked up as we entered. "Mr. Clinkscale?" she inquired.

"Yes, ma'am."

"Come right this way. Mr. Capola is expecting you."

Again he was very gracious as he greeted me and met Paulette. "I'm excited about your material," he said as he nodded his head toward the familiar-looking cassettes on his desk. "In a couple of weeks we will have available a weekly slot of open air time. Someone's contract will have run out and they are unable to renew it at the present time. Would you like to fill that slot?"

Would I? "Why... why, yes, sir! I'll give it a try!" I said as I glanced toward Paulette who was nodding her approval. We signed a contract and shook hands.

"What will the name of your program be?" he asked me.

"Why...why, I'm not sure. I...I haven't had time to think about it," I answered, still in a daze.

"Think it over tonight, Lonnie. You can call us tomorrow and let us know what you decide."

That evening when I was alone I thought, My life has been touched by so many people like Mr. James Rozzi, Miss Thelma Barnes, Mr. Albert Marinelli, Miss Irma Davis. They took time out of their busy schedules to love me and be concerned about me. I should allow God to touch the lives of others through me just as He used those fine people and many others to touch and change mine. The program should be called "Touch Somebody's Life Ministries."

After two years of broadcasting, at the time Lonette was born, I took time off to help Paulette care for our fragile little daughter. When she was about a year old, I decided to approach WBBW, a radio station with a wider audience, and try to use the same format I had used on the Christian station, hoping I could reach more people with the Christian message.

I talked by phone with the manager. "Sounds interesting," he said. "Bring some of your material in and we'll listen to it."

Through the listeners of both stations I received letters, phone calls and requests for additional speaking engagements and discovered, to my pleasure, that my speeches were helping people.

One was entitled "They Shall Be One Flesh," based on Genesis 2:23-24: "And Adam said, This (woman) is now bone of my bones, and flesh of my flesh: she shall be called Woman, because she was taken out of Man. Therefore shall a man leave his father and his mother, and shall cleave unto his wife: and they will be one flesh."

I pointed out how many marriages were ending in divorce and how divorce destroys the family unit. "The devil is fighting marriages," I told my unseen audience. "Never before have I seen so many saints applying for divorce. It troubled me so, that I asked the Lord, 'What is going on? Has the church become so busy with less important issues that she is not taking the time to help troubled marriages?'"

While I prepared for that broadcast, the Lord showed me that because the husband and wife have their own minds and personalities and, in many cases, have been brought up in very different environments, misunderstandings are inevitable. The Word of God very specifically describes the responsibility of both the husband and the wife, but the churches have become so modernized that such topics are no longer taught from the Scriptures.

In preparation for that broadcast I interviewed several people, asking them, "When you got married did you and your spouse have counseling or teaching about marriage? When you had problems, were there any programs within the church to help you?" I learned that only a few churches require an engaged couple to attend extensive counseling or seminars about marriage and fewer teach their members how to maintain the roles of homemaker and provider.

I warned my radio audience, "The devil will do all he can to destroy the marriage, even though marriage is sanctioned by the Lord." I stated that independence and stubbornness, lack of respect, immaturity, influence of friends and family members cause many marital problems.

I advised my listeners, "If you have a problem, you must learn to get down on your knees and ask the Lord for guidance. Learn to pray and fast. Always seek the Lord in decision-making. By putting the Lord first in your marriage, you will be able to become one in God."

Shortly after the program was over, a young mother of four children phoned me. "My church does not believe in divorce," she said, "but my husband constantly threatens to harm our children and me. I feel I should leave him for our safety, but my pastor insists that it would be wrong to leave. I feel like I am a slave to a very unpleasant and dangerous situation."

I told her that in times of life-threatening situations a wife often has to separate from her husband for safety's sake. "Listen to God, not a man," I advised and prayed for her to receive guidance from the Lord.

She found the courage to leave her husband and has started to attend church services again, has gone back to school, and now holds a good job.

A young married man, who was ruining his marriage as a result of watching X-rated movies on television at nights after his wife went to sleep, happened to turn on his radio on his way to work just as I was saying, "I am not against all cable TV, however I am against the pornography that is shown, because it is destroying society and polluting our minds with filth. It is stripping us of our morals and our relationship with God." That day I was speaking on "The Lust of Pornography."

"My heart is troubled this morning," I continued, "because we have become so lustful that we will do anything to satisfy our burning lust. We say it is wrong for a man or a woman to commit a sex-related crime, but it is all right for them to go to X-rated movies and all right for the TV networks to show those filthy movies. It's all right to sell Hustler and Playboy.

"Newsweek magazine reports that Americans buy an estimated two million tickets to X-rated films, resulting in an annual box office intake of about 500 million dollars. Many have become overtaken with pornography and have committed sexual crimes to satisfy their lusts.

"My friend, God is watching you. If you do not change your wicked ways you will feel the wrath of God. The lust demon has told you it is all right to look at pornography. You are still alive today only by the mercy of God.

"Many of you don't want to be delivered because you are so caught up in your sinful ways. You have no business watching violence or anything that is geared toward sex, whether it is a soap opera or an X-rated movie. It's time for you to turn that filth off."

The young man who was listening to my broadcast suddenly realized he had a serious problem that he couldn't overcome on his own. He stopped driving and asked God for help. Several weeks later he phoned me to tell me what had taken place, explaining, "I was so hooked that my wife had to leave me, but now, through counseling and prayer, I am gradually being helped."

Several people received their salvation after hearing my presentation "The Nightmare," a talk I prepared after I had dreamed that Jesus had returned according to the prophecies in Scripture. After my broadcast entitled "Cast Your Fate to the Wind," urging families to care for and love our senior citizens, an elderly lady called, weeping. She told me, "I'm so glad to hear a young person cares and is willing to take a stand."

Because I have often stressed the importance of completing high school, numerous young people where I work have come to me and said, "Lonnie, I have enrolled in the GED class." One 55-year-old man announced to me, "I'm going to get my diploma. I just wanted to let you know."

Through the leading of the Lord I have prepared more than fifty different speeches, including such topics as teen-age suicide, blaming others for our own mistakes, child abuse, and the neglect of our senior citizens. God does work through his willing servants. The Scriptures tell us we are to be like a light on a hill. That is so very true.

The Lord has recently blessed Touch Somebody's Life Ministries to be a nonprofit organization which helps disadvantaged people. Funds generated through my speaking engagements are used to help the elderly pay their utility bills, the person who wants to go into business for himself, or a child who needs a new pair of tennis shoes. I can't help much, but it's my way of saying to people in need, "Hey, I'm supporting you. I'm backing you. I love you and understand the hard times you're having."

Having been without love and understanding and many material needs during my childhood years has made me sharply aware of the needs of others. I am especially sensitive to the problems of the elderly and teens. Young people are our only hope for tomorrow, but the only way they can be successful is by learning from the older generation who have too often been pushed aside.

Preparing the broadcasts, the increased public speaking engagements that have resulted and the opportunities for ministry which follow each presentation have often been more time consuming and draining than I would have liked, but I can honestly say it's been worth it all. And I am grateful for the love and support of an understanding wife.

Our youngest daughter Crystal

Chapter 19
Up the Ladder

In late 1988, shortly after Paulette and I learned we were expecting a second child, I began to dream about becoming a supervisor in the hospital. Mr. Smith started to ask me to fill in for him when he went on vacation or had a day off and I realized the Lord might be preparing me for such a position. Even though several employees had more seniority than I, Mr. Smith seemed to appreciate my sincerity and the fact that I rarely missed a day's work. Whenever he asked me to work extra hours or take over for him, I made every effort to do more than was expected of me.

Mr. Smith began to spend more time teaching me various facets of his job. "Lonnie, here's the pager. Let's see how you handle this situation."

Many times when I became discouraged, Mr. Smith assumed the role of father. Each time I talked with him he gave me sound advice. I valued his frequent "Lonnie, don't be discouraged. Everything will be okay." Mr. Smith often came to my speaking engagements.

Although he looked after me, I was expected to perform my duties at work just like the other employees and received no special privileges.

Often when management courses were made available through the hospital, Mr. Smith got in touch with Sister Renee, the nun who was over the inservice training department, then talked with the director of housekeeping, recommending, "I feel this young man should be included in some of the hospital's management courses. He's not a supervisor yet, but I believe we should start training him."

I attended many management courses as the only non-supervisor present. There was no guarantee that I would get a promotion, but the experience and learning finally paid off.

When an opening for a supervisory position became available, I applied but did not receive it. It was not long until another supervisory position became available, and again I was turned down. I can recall going home that night feeling very discouraged.

I went to my knees and said to the Lord, "Why didn't I receive that job? Lord, you know I needed that job in order to support my family. You know Paulette isn't able to work right now. She will need to stay home and take care of our expected baby."

The Lord spoke to me. "Haven't I given you everything you have asked for? Haven't I told you that as long as you put Me first in your life I will bless you? You must learn to have faith in Me, and patience. You will receive a supervisor's job in My own timing."

Paulette went back to work, transferring to Medical Intensive, a high-stress area. I was concerned that the work might be too much for her at that time. "Maybe it's time for you to go back to school," I suggested.

"Lonnie, I like working there," she told me, "because I can talk with the families and give them comfort and encouragement. I need to wait until our expected child comes before I go back to school."

I continued to check the bulletin board in our department every day to see if there were any new job openings. One day I discovered an opening for a supervisor in the housekeeping department (Environmental Services) had been posted. I went directly to Mr. Smith's office.

"There's an opening for a supervisor in our department?" I asked him.

"Yes, Lonnie. One of the supervisors had been moved up to

another position."

Immediately I applied with the secretary of our department and began to pray for the Lord's guidance. He instructed me to get some anointing oil and anoint the bottom of my shoes and my hands, then walk into the housekeeping office and anoint the supervisor's vacant desk where I wished to sit.

The anointing is most important. We don't fully understand, but know that according to the Scriptures the anointing is powerful if you follow every instruction the Lord gives you. I did as the Lord instructed me to do.

That following week I received a call from the personnel department stating that I was to have two interviews, one with the director of the housekeeping department and another with the associate housekeeping director. During my prayer times at home, the Lord began to work with me through several Scriptures He brought to my remembrance and instructed me that before the interviews I was to anoint my hands with oil again and He would bless me with the job.

The Lord also told me that all I had to do was open my mouth and He would give me the words to say. I breathed a prayer of thankfulness to God that I no longer had to dread speaking to anyone, because my problem of stuttering had never returned.

I had no idea how to answer some of the questions pertaining to supervision which the director and associate director asked me, but the Lord gave me the wisdom to know how to respond to the questions from the experience I had received under the guidance of Mr. Smith.

Two weeks later, after I was notified by the Personel Department that I had been selected for the position, the Director of Environmental Services came into the area I was cleaning. He approached me and held out his hand. "Lonnie, I want to congratulate you. You have been selected to be one of the four supervisors in our department. I look forward to working with you." I shook his hand with enthusiasm and thanked him. The words "Do what I say and I will bless you with the job" echoed in my mind.

As I cleaned the Personnel Director's office, he too announced how happy he was that I had been accepted.

That same night, John Smith, my supervisor, with tears in his eyes, grabbed me and hugged me. "Lonnie, I'm so happy for you! I can remember when you first came in as a young lad through the OWE program in 1978, and I'm so glad God used me to have a part in selecting you as an OWE worker. Now look at you! You're on the same level as I am! I know you're going to do well. If there's anything I can do to help you, I will." It was an emotional moment.

The Lord had used the long wait for my promotion to teach me patience, because He knew I would need a lot in my new position. I was responsible for forty employees, for the cleaning of three general floors— the third level which included cleaning surgery, recovery, emergency and patient rooms, as well as the fifth and the sixth levels. I was responsible for resolving any complaints, making sure the employee's concerns would be heard and addressed and that the best of care would be provided for patients and visitors alike. I was grateful to receive that responsibility because I knew through it the Lord would prepare me for something else. I knew with His help I could handle the job as well as my college classes and my family responsibilities.

I thanked the Lord that through the years He had taught me how to study and manage my time. I had learned to allow Him to set the guidelines. "Lonnie, if you will do this...that... you will have time to study, spend time at church and time with your family."

The Lord also taught me that He was my Provider. Even though my wife had been off work for a while, there was never a bill left unpaid and always plenty of food in our house. He taught me how to manage every dollar I had.

Sometimes we'd panic, wondering how we were going to make it financially. But God would always remind us, "You can do all things through Christ who strengthens you. Walk with Me every day and there will be no need to panic."

I learned to fellowship with the Lord throughout each day, from the moment I awoke until I fell asleep. This was something I had often heard about and read in the Scriptures, but had never fully understood until I put it into practice.

After working as a supervisor for one and a half years I began to have the desire to become one of the four administrative coordinators at the hospital. Persons in these positions represent administration during the off-shift hours. The administrative coordinator is highly respected, has a lot of authority and makes many important decisions. It is one of the highest positions bestowed upon a hospital employee.

One day while in prayer I told the Lord, "I'm very grateful for the supervisory position you've blessed me with, but I feel You have something more for me." I began to study the Scriptures and listen.

Through His written and spoken Word the Lord asked me, "What are the desires of your heart?"

"I would like to become an administrative coordinator. I want to represent You, Lord, as a walking testimony to what You can do when a person trusts in You. I want people to know how You took a slow learner who was bound in the chains of illiteracy and set him free through Your Word and Your power."

From that day on, I often thought, "Lord, the blessing of this new position would be similar to the blessing of Joseph in the Bible. The Lord delivered Joseph from prison in the land of Egypt to make him the trustee of the whole land."

The Lord told me, "I will bless you with that position within two weeks."

Just two weeks later, a notice was placed on the employee bulletin board that administration was looking for a part-time administrative coordinator to work 16 hours a week. The Lord instructed me, "Lonnie, apply for the position even though you will be taking a drastic cut in pay."

If accepted, I would be going from a 40-hour-per-week position as supervisor, which paid very well, to a two-day-a-week position. The Lord assured me that if I would step out in faith and obedience, He would supply my needs.

When I applied for the position, the person who processes all applications looked up at me with astonishment. "Lonnie, do you realize this job is for only two days a week?" I nodded that I understood. "You lose all your benefits. Everything. Do you understand that?"

"Yes, I understand. This is what I want to do." I could not feel dismayed because the Lord had told me, "Lonnie, you will be provided for and you will not be part time. You WILL be able to pay all your bills. In fact, you will be earning more than you are now. You and your family will not lack anything. Walk by faith." By faith I filled out the application.

Once again I was instructed by the Lord to anoint my hands and the bottoms of my feet before I went in to be interviewed. He assured me that regardless of the many applicants who had applied for the position I would receive the job and receive more hours than had been posted. I had no trouble in believing the Lord, because throughout my life He had never forsaken me. He always keeps His word.

On the day of the interview, the Lord told me that when I met with the executive officer, He would speak through me, giving me the correct responses, even though I did not know much about hospital policy and procedures.

Although I was a little tense when I walked into the room and closed the door behind me, the executive's personality and approach made me feel comfortable, so I knew that God was in charge of the interview. I did not feel the least bit intimidated.

After the chief executive officer interviewed other applicants I was informed that I had been selected to become administrative coordinator of the twelfth-largest hospital in the state of Ohio and, as far as I am concerned, the best hospital in the nation. I give glory and honor to the Lord for what He has done in my life.

Who would have ever thought that a dummy, the slowest kid in elementary school, a kid with a severe speaking impairment, the young man who was told that he would never make it in this life and certainly could never excel in college, would be a high school grad, a college grad, a public speaker, author of a book and an administrative co-ordinator of one of the biggest hospitals in the state of Ohio?

Chapter 20
More Than I Could Ask
or Imagine

"You've got to be crazy!" several of my fellow hospital employees told me. "You've got two daughters, a wife, a house to pay for and you're going to apply for a job that's for only two days a week?"

"I'll be taken care of through faith," I assured them.

Paulette, who was working only part time, said, "Lonnie, I hope you know what you're doing."

"I've discussed it with the Lord and with our pastor," I told her. "I feel the purpose of the pastor is to keep in close touch with God in order to give his people counsel. After praying our pastor concluded, 'Brother Clinkscale, we've both prayed. Go for it! We have to trust God.' So don't worry, Paulette, I've saved some money back in case we need it."

My wife heaved a sigh of approval. "Well, Lonnie, if God is in it, I'm in it."

When I was selected for the position in administration, the Lord blessed me to be able to work two days a week as Administrative Coordinator and two days as Environmental Services Supervisor until the hospital could find someone to fill my position. By the time they filled the vacancy, I had been trained sufficiently to work full time in administration. The Lord blessed me to work 32 hours instead of sixteen, which meant I worked only four days a week but made nearly twice as much money as I had earned as Environmental Services Supervisor. I never got a chance to work part time.

The Lord had kept His word. We never needed to use the money I had saved. God made the way because we were willing to step out in faith.

About six months ago, while at work, I met the teacher who had advised me to join the Army instead of considering college. Her mother was a patient at St. Elizabeth's. The moment I saw her, the familiar words rang in my memory, "Lonnie, you'll never make it in college." Her eyes grew large as she stared at my familiar face.perched gracefully above a suit and necktie. I sensed that she was surprised to see that my goals and dreams were being accomplished. I also sensed she realized that she had made a mistake.

"Lonnie! How are you?" She could not take her eyes off the clothes I wore, the apparel of a professional man.

I told her, "I have completed the labor classes at Youngstown State and am only ten hours short of completing the four-year communications program." She forced a smile, trying to hide her thinking, "Wow, a miracle has happened!"
God has blessed me more than I could ever ask or imagine. He has healed my mind and my speech, filled my life with His love and acceptance, blessed me with a loving and faith-ful wife and two beautiful healthy daughters, a college edu-cation and a good job. My heart's desire is to praise Him and please Him in everything I do.

Chapter 21
My Advice

I have often been asked, "Lonnie, are you the exception?" My reply is always the same: "I believe that with God there are no exceptions. When you put God first in your life, regardless what type of learning disability you have, God will bring you through."

My message to slow learners or those with a learning disability is this: The key to your success in overcoming your learning disabilities is accepting the Lord Jesus Christ as your Lord and Savior and putting Him first in all things. You must have faith that you can do all things in Christ who strengthens you. You must never let people intimidate you. You must not be hooked into believing that you will not excel because of the environment in which you live or because you are being brought up in a single-parent home.

Every day before you attend class, ask the Lord to go with you into the classroom. Ask Him to open up your mind and to give you a clear understanding of the information you are about to receive. Also, before you take an exam, spend a few moments to pray a silent prayer, asking for His help.

At the end of each school day ask the Lord to help you to remember what you have been taught and to help you complete any homework assignments. After you have completed your exam or your homework, take a moment to thank the Lord for what He has done and what He is about to do in your life.

You must believe without a shadow of a doubt that you are not so dumb that you cannot learn if you study with His help. And you are not so smart that you will learn if you do not study.

If you perceive it and believe it, then you can achieve it.

Parents, convince your children that they can learn if they put their minds to it. Do not discourage them if they do not do as well as other children. Do not become angry and scold them because they are having a hard time comprehending the materials. This only makes a child nervous and causes him to withdraw within himself, fearing to open up to his teachers or his parents, fearing that he will be rejected.

If a child makes some progress, even if he only receives a C or a D, that child should be rewarded for his efforts while being encouraged, "You can do better." Parents should praise the Lord for what He has done and for what He is about to do.

Take the time to see why the child is having a hard time comprehending. Become active in your child's school. Go to the parent/teacher meetings. If your child needs to attend some type of remedial class, instead of adding to his feeling that he is a dummy, explain to him the positive reasons for attending these classes. Take the time to help the child with his homework.

Most important of all, before you help your child, both parents and the child should go before the Lord in prayer. Ask Him to open up your mind and your child's mind as you prepare to study and to help him complete his homework assignments. Let your child know he is special and that the Lord loves him.

Seek tutoring for your child in subjects with which you are not familiar. Some community agencies provide free tutoring to students and their parents. To find them, check with your school or your local Board of Education. Perhaps you as a parent should take a couple of lessons on how various courses are taught in the school system.

Parents must make sure their children are not in a hostile environment where mom and dad are constantly fighting each other. It is very difficult for a child to learn in school when mom and dad are not getting along at home.

Parents should also make sure their children have a well-balanced breakfast before school and a good well-balanced evening meal before the child retires for the day.

A parent must never compare a child who has a learning disability with a child who is smarter. Never make such statements as, "You will never be anything in life because you are too dumb. You will be like your Uncle Bob who is in jail, or like your Aunt Lucy who got pregnant at the age of fourteen." These statements may damage a child for life or take years for a child to overcome.

Finally, now is a good time for parents who have not graduated from school or from college to get back into school and realize that you can do all things through Christ who strengthens you. (Philippians 4:13) Realize that you and your child are somebody in God.

I hope the following poem, gives both students and their parents encouragement.

I'm Somebody
by Irma L. Corbett

By the grace of God, I am what I want to be.
I've been blessed with love and hope and dignity.
Some day I hope this world can be proud of me,
All because I'm somebody and want to be.
To be somebody and that somebody to be me
Is more than a mere thought, you see.
It takes self-discipline, experience and liberty
To make being somebody a reality.

I live not in wealth or poverty,
And the role of a scum or a bum is not for me,
Nor am I a threat or a nuisance to society.
I'm somebody because I want to be.
I remember when I could have been nobody, you see.
But I said to myself, "That is not what I want to be."
Then I set my goal toward a high morality.
That's why I'm somebody and that somebody is me.

Somebody can be you, and you can be somebody, too,
By starting now to make your life anew,
By telling beyond and despair that you are through—
All because you are somebody and that somebody is you.

* * *

This poem, written by my wife, shares our feelings as we look back on our lives both alone and together.

It's Been Worth It All

It's been worth it all— every tear that's been shed,
All the tests and trials I used to dread;
The pain of saying, "When will it all be over?"
You were there. I didn't really see You then,
But that's what I had to discover.
No matter how heavy the load became,
Jesus, You were always the same.
Your tender, loving kindness led the way.
How else could I explain?
The Power of Your Spirit took my mind
When I felt I'd lose my grip.
You stood before me with open arms
When I felt as though my feet would surely slip.
It's been worth it all to see Your hand move in my life,
And feel the peace of mind You breathe on me,
Removing all envy and strife

So, to look back on the me before and after,
Jesus, I've found love in You.
My heart is now filled with laughter.
I want so much to please this great God I serve
For what He's done for me;
I know it's nothing I deserve.
There's been time I know that I have failed,
Missed the mark,
But Your blood covered me. It prevailed.
It's been worth it all
To receive You and every blessing that has followed.
Yes, I can stand straight and tall.
That's why I know for a certainty—
It's been worth it;
It's been worth it all!

HEY, DUMMY!

An Inspirational Testimony for Success

by
Lonnie Clinkscale
With Melva Libb

Second Printing — April 1994

1

Cover Portrait: Jeannie Robbins
ISBN 0-9640311-0-8 (previously ISBN 0-936369-44-2)
Copyright © 1994 by Lonnie Clinkscale
Clinkscale Publications and Productions, Inc.
P.O. Box 5696, Youngstown, Ohio 44504